George S. 4th Duke of Marlborough

The Marlborough gems

being a collection of works in cameo and intaglio formed by George, third duke of Marlborough / catalogued with descriptions, and an introduction by M. H. Nevil Story-Maskelyne.

George S. 4th Duke of Marlborough

The Marlborough gems
being a collection of works in cameo and intaglio formed by George, third duke of Marlborough / catalogued with descriptions, and an introduction by M. H. Nevil Story-Maskelyne.

ISBN/EAN: 9783741195785

Manufactured in Europe, USA, Canada, Australia, Japa

Cover: Foto ©ninafisch / pixelio.de

Manufactured and distributed by brebook publishing software (www.brebook.com)

George S. 4th Duke of Marlborough

The Marlborough gems

INTRODUCTION.

THE collection of cameos and intaglios of which this little volume is a Catalogue, has for nearly a century deservedly possessed a wide reputation. The two splendid volumes printed and distributed by the third Duke of Marlborough in 1780 and 1791, wherein a hundred of the most remarkable pieces in his collection were described and figured, would alone have sufficed to establish this fame for the "Marlborough Gems." To the archæologist, however, the cabinet at Blenheim has always possessed an additional and a singular interest, from its including the collection of gems that had been formed by that famous Earl of Arundel who, during the troubled times of the first Charles, found a solace for the abridgment of his dignities in collecting works of art and monuments of antiquity.

The Arundel Gems, however, formed only one part of the great collection of works in cameo and intaglio brought together by George, third Duke of Marlborough; nor were gems the only, though probably they were the favourite, objects that he collected. The paintings on the walls of Blenheim Palace would alone suffice to illustrate the splendid tastes of this "magnificent" Duke; tastes for the gratification of which an accumulated fortune, and the condition of Europe, offered him a rare opportunity.

Among the pictures at Blenheim there is one famous canvas on which Sir Joshua Reynolds has handed down to us the portrait of the third Duke, his Duchess, and their elder children. In his hand his Grace holds a large cameo, and at his side stands his son the Marquis of Blandford, afterwards of White Knights celebrity, carrying under his arm a red morocco case; one of the ten similar cases that still contain the collection of gems. This gem-case serves at once to introduce a mass of effective colour into the picture, and to complete the motive of the scene by presenting to us the Duke in his character of a gem collector.

The particular cameo he holds is that numbered 390 in this Catalogue; it was one of the gems collected individually by the Duke's excellent taste, and it no doubt claimed on that account, no less than from its high intrinsic importance, a place of honour among his gems.

The proportion which the part of the Collection thus formed by the Duke, by separate purchases in Italy and at home, bears to the whole of the Cabinet, amounts to about the half.

The remaining half is composed of two distinct collections united by the Duke to his own, each of which was important and celebrated.

The one has already been alluded to as formed, in the early half of the century previous to that in which the Duke was a collector, by the illustrious Thomas Howard, Earl of Arundel, the Mæcenas of the Caroline period; the other was brought together by William, second Earl of Bessborough, and third Viscount Duncannon, a nobleman some thirty years senior to the third Duke, who had no doubt cultivated his taste, and in part formed his collection of gems during a period of travel on the Continent, which terminated in 1739, the same year in which the third Duke of Marlborough was born.

Of the two collections which thus became blended with the third Duke's acquisitions, to shine with united lustre as "the Marlborough Gems," the first to demand a notice is that formed by Lord Arundel. Alike from the character of its contents and from its authentic pedigree, the Arundelian Collection stands now almost alone in interest. One has only to consider how very few of the existing gem collections in Europe were in being before the beginning of the last century, and what confusion was introduced into the study of gems as records of the past, by the forgeries and fabrications carried on chiefly in Italy during that century, in order to recognise the value that must needs attach to a collection formed at the date when a Stuart sovereign held in abeyance the ducal rank of the proud and accomplished head of the house of Howard. In the midst of such a collection we stand so far at least on solid ground, that we may feel sure of every gem with a classical subject that we examine belonging either to the ages of Greek or Roman art, or to that long-after age in which the classical arts were revivified and seemed to burst forth into a sort of preternatural rejuvenescence. But the gem-engraver of the Revival never or seldom copied slavishly the works of antiquity; he aspired to convey their sentiment, but with a freedom of treatment to which, in fact,

INTRODUCTION.

whatever was noble in the Renaissance school was due. He perfected his technical methods, and in this respect could challenge the finest works of Roman artists. That his hand never acquired the subtle and spontaneous cunning, or his spirit the simply grand conception of the Greek masters, is only to say that as " Greece was living Greece no more," so, too, the myths of that once living Greece were dead. The comparison of the gems of the cinque-cento or Renaissance school, is therefore rather to be made with those that were called into existence during the Roman Revival of art, under Hadrian and the Antonines, than with the gems of the ages when Greek art flourished on its own soil, or had been freshly imported into Imperial Rome.

It is more particularly with the gems of the latter class that the works of the last century sought to compete, and sought too often to compete, not in freedom of design and its attendant freedom of treatment, but by simply bringing an improved and in fact almost perfect technical method to bear in multiplying copies of antique originals.

From such gems as these, then, the Arundelian cases were entirely free. Unfortunately—perhaps at the time their handsome mountings were given them by the founder of the collection, or more probably in accordance with the mischievous fashion of the last century—the very noblest and best of these Arundelian gems have suffered at the hands of the polisher. To remove by a few turns of a wheel that slight dimming of the ancient lustre which Time has wrought, or, as it were, breathed like a subtle film over the surface, is an easy task. But with that wiping away of the breath of Time, there goes not only the evidence of venerable age, but, too often, the most delicate and artistic characteristics of the outline : a new surface and a new outline are left in place of those the artist gave, and the degrees of relief of different parts of the subject are modified. Several of the Arundelian gems have certainly suffered much from this cause, but nevertheless the collection remains an invaluable illustration of the gem-engraver's art as it was known in the earlier half of the 17th century ; for Lord Arundel's life of sixty years ended in 1646.

The gems—and we may presume the whole of them—were included in the portion of Lord Arundel's property that descended to his son and successor, Henry Frederick Lord Maltravers, and from him they passed to the sixth Duke of Norfolk, his son—the Duke to whom Oxford is indebted for one portion of the Arundelian Marbles. His son, the seventh Duke, succeeded to the possession of them ; but now, by a strange fate, they passed away from the House of Howard : for the Arundelian antiquities, including the gems, were retained as her property by the divorced Duchess, that Lady Mary Mordaunt who, in 1705, five years after the decree for her divorce was passed in the House of Lords, died and bequeathed the whole of her estate to her husband, Sir John Germain. She had previously sold the other antiquities; but the gems passed to Sir John under her will.

In 1718, Sir John married for his second wife the Lady Elizabeth Berkeley, daughter of Charles, second Earl of Berkeley, and by his will he left that lady in possession of all his property.

Thus the Arundelian Cabinet of Gems passed by a second step of alienation from Arundel Castle into the possession of Sir John's widow, the Lady Elizabeth Germain. There seems no reason to suppose that during these changes of ownership the collection had been despoiled of any of its treasures; so that we may fairly presume that Lady Elizabeth possessed it much in the state in which it was left by the noble connoisseur who formed it. And, fortunately, we have a valuable and trustworthy record of the contents of the collection at this time in a catalogue, a copy of which, in manuscript, dated 1727, exists in the library of the Society of Antiquaries. The "Lady Betty" survived till 1769; but in October, 1762, her great niece, the Lady Mary Beauclerk, was married to Lord Charles Spencer, brother of the third Duke of Marlborough. This lady was the daughter of Lord Vere Beauclerk, created Lord Vere of Hanworth, who subsequently became fourth Duke of St. Albans, and whose wife was Mary Chambers, daughter and heiress of Thomas Chambers, Esq., of Hanworth, and Lady Mary, his wife, sister to Lady Elizabeth Germain.

From her great aunt Lady Elizabeth, the Lady Mary Beauclerk, the bride of 1762, received the gems—a splendid gift. Perhaps gems were looked on as a sort of bridal appanage descending as a casket of family jewels might have descended in each successive generation to the lady through whose alliance a family hoped to be perpetuated: such, at least, seems to have been the case with the bequest of the Hunsdon gems at Berkeley Castle in 1603.

By a family arrangement, however, the Arundelian Collection now passed from the hands of Lady Mary Spencer to add to the magnificence, and embellish with a fresh archæological value, the collection which the Duke, her brother-in-law, was at that time busy in forming. And it had now, after its various alienations of ownership, passed into a haven of rest, in which, for above a century, it has lain undisturbed. Once, indeed, some seven years before the gems had reached this final destination, they had been offered by Lady Elizabeth to the trustees of

INTRODUCTION.   ix

the then nascent British Museum for the great sum of £10,000. The offer was not accepted. This sum, however, if the collection was still entire, must have been much below what it had originally cost; for the Earl of Arundel is declared by Evelyn to have given that very sum for a collection of gems that he purchased of Daniel Nys, of Venice; and Evelyn himself was employed by the Earl in collecting such objects in Rome and other parts of Italy.

On examining the Arundelian Collection, one is struck with the considerable number of the gems that are not antique. In cameos of large size and importance it is rich, and it is particularly so in such as are of a size adapted for a finger ring, but, as we should expect, many of these are of the Medicean age. To this age we are compelled to refer the beautiful cameo (No. 160)—the nuptials of Cupid and Psyche; a gem better known, perhaps, and more often copied in various materials, than any other in any collection. To this time, also, are referable two of the earliest examples (Nos. 201 and 325) of the shell cameos which, from the facility of their execution and the cheapness both of their material and workmanship, have almost extinguished the art of the cameo engraver on hard stones in our age. Among the antique cameos particularly important from their sizes and subjects must be noticed the interesting suite of great cameo portraits of Imperial personages: such are the Antonia (No. 414); the admirable cameo of Agrippina (No. 416); the two busts of Claudius (Nos. 422 and 423); the bust of the uncle of Trajan (No. 452); the Faustina (No. 466); the Commodus (No. 480); and the two cameos, so remarkable, for the age to which they belong, of Julia Paula and Julia Mammæa (Nos. 495 and 496); and to these may still be added the Elagabalus (No. 494); and the bust, possibly of Julia Mæsa (No. 557).

As an illustration of earliest Renaissance, or even pre-Renaissance work, the singular little gem engraved on ruby or ruby spinel—the crowned portrait of Charles cinq, king of France, No. 583 of this Catalogue, is most remarkable; as its date must have been early in the second half of the 14th century.* Among the important intaglios of

---

* That gems were engraved at so early a date is proved by an observation of Mr. King's, to whom I am indebted for the light thrown on the date of this gem, while this work is passing through the press. Mr. King observes, in confirmation of this ruby being the actual signet of Charles, how Ammonato, in his "History of Florence" (p. 741), mentions that Peruzzi the Florentine *singolare intagliatore di pietre* forged the seal of Durazzo in the year 1379.

b

the Arundelian Cabinet, we may instance a famous gem (No. 341), the Rape of the Palladium, from the Trojan Temple:—

> Impius ex quo
> Tydides sed enim, scelerumque inventor Ulysses,
> Fatale adgressi sacrato avellere templo
> Palladium, caesis summae custodibus arcis,
> Corripuere sacram effigiem.

The signature of the artist, Felix, and the name, probably of the owner, Calpurnius Severus, have, of course, not passed unchallenged by the scepticism of critics. Here, however, the pedigree of the Arundel collection comes in as important evidence to rescue this gem from the charge of being a modern fabrication, while the peculiar form of the inscriptions on it is hardly compatible with its being a cinque-cento forgery. The Medusa on a sapphire (No. 98); the marvellously fine intaglio portrait (No. 122) of Marcia, or some lady of an earlier time, on a sardine, as remarkable for its magnitude as for its fine execution, in a style that we can scarcely attribute to the artists of the Renaissance; the beautifully designed little Bacchus on a beryl (No. 183), injured, alas! by a vigorous repolishing of the stone; the noble intaglio bust of Mars (No. 109); the fine cameo representing Ariadne (No. 194), may be cited among the more exquisite of the antique works that had a place with the Arundelian Gems.

The MS. catalogue of the Arundelian Gems that has been alluded to as existing in the library of the Society of Antiquaries (No. 43, Smart Lethieullier), is a copy from an original catalogue "lent by the Right Honourable the Lady Betty Jermain, owner of the cabinet." That original, no doubt, passed with the gems into the possession of the Duke of Marlborough; and on it, and on Natter's catalogue of the Bessborough gems, his Grace founded a catalogue, which, besides giving an account of the Arundel and Bessborough collections, was to embrace the descriptions of the gems of his own private collection. But this catalogue, which was to have been printed, seems never to have been completed. Copies in manuscript, in various stages of progress, remain, and in some of these the original descriptions of the Arundel catalogue are simply copied, the Italian addenda to the latter being converted into Latin.

The title of the MS. at Somerset House is as follows:—

Gemmae incisae excisaeque, maximâ ex parte antiquae, quas coelatura insignes, auroque ornatas ingens copia, multiplex color, magnitudo

INTRODUCTION. xi

lapidum sculptorum mirabilis et prorsus inimitabilis ars summopere commēdant.

Thesaurus olim Arundellianus primis Europæ cimeliis sane invidendus qui nunc in Ædibus nobilis Matronæ D^{nac} Elizabethæ Germain, Londini summâ curâ servatur.

The catalogue from which this is a transcript was, however, itself a copy, made by some Italian hand, probably not far from the date of the transcript, 1727; and to this copyist certain Italian notices, completing the descriptions, were due. The allusion to Stosch's work at the end of the description of the gem (Thec. E. No. 2), the Rape of the Palladium (No. 341 of this volume), and also in the account of the cameo No. 160, is sufficient to show that the Italian annotator did not write till after 1724.

The more remote original was undoubtedly a true Arundelian Catalogue, describing the gems as they originally stood in the cabinet of Lord Arundel. Indeed, a note at the end of the MS. at Somerset House records it to have been: "Estratto del' antico catalogo delle Gemme intagliate, e scolpite, che furono gia il tresoro piu riguardévole del famosissimo Museo Arondelliano, le quali quasi tutte legate in oro, che monta al valore di piu che quatro cento-cinquanta doppie. Sono conservate in cinque casette notate con le lettere A, B, C, D, E, con un ragguaglio piu distinto et esatto delle differenza accidentáli di quelle."

The Catalogue contains the description of 263 gems, arranged in the five cases; 133 being intaglios, and 130 cameos. The descriptions are in Latin; an Italian addition, already alluded to, descriptive of the stone, and often also of the setting, being appended to the account of each gem.* What number of these 263 gems is now contained in the

---

* An illustration of the manner in which these descriptions are given may be quoted in the case of one of the most conspicuous works of art in this cabinet. It refers to the gem already alluded to (No. 160), the well-known lovely cameo representing Cupid and Psyche in hymeneal procession. It is the seventh gem in the "*Theca quarta*" of Lady Elizabeth's catalogue. "Psyches et Cupidinis nuptiæ TPYΦΩN EΠOIEI, in onice di fondo ben negro, scultura di bianco bruno, coperta d'oro smaltato, per la quale sola ó stata piu volte offerta la somma di cinque cento Lire sterline, che montano a piu di due mila scudi, che perciò il possessore di detta onice e pronto a rabattere le 500 lire ogni qual volta gli sia permesso da chi fara l'acquisto di tutto il resto." Vide Spon. Miscellanea eruditæ Antiquitatis, pag. 9; et Stoschii gemmas antiquas, pag. 94. These additions seem thus to have been made with a view to a catalogue for a sale.

cases at Blenheim it is difficult with precision to say, as it is not in every case possible to identify them with certainty under the fanciful descriptions given of them in the old catalogue. There can, however, be little doubt as to the identification of some 235 of them. The remainder, which that difficult kind of scrutiny, the comparison of things described with the descriptions of them given in no definite order, has not, even with great labour, enabled us to identify, amount to eight intaglios, and twenty cameos. Of these, several certainly are no longer among the Marlborough Gems.* Whether they were ejected or changed for others by the Duke, or had been removed for use as ornaments before the Collection passed into his hands, it may be impossible now to ascertain. We may instance the following as occurring in the Catalogue among the subjects that could not be so disguised under any peculiarities of their attribution as not to be recognisable when sought for in the Collection as it stands.†

Theca A. 39. Quinque facies imberbes, totidemque barbatæ si spectentur inversæ. *Corniola.* 2.

A representation of this often-repeated conceit of the Renaissance artist is seen at the back of the Bessborough gem No. 255 in this volume.

Theca B. 38. Caput Servatoris nostri Jesu X^{ti}.—*In pietra verde nefritica, chiamata altrimente Giadro. Cinta d'oro.* 2.

,, ,, 39. Ecce Homo.—*In Diaspro verde con macchie di sangue. Cinta d'oro.* 3.

,, D. 17. Servator nostri Jesu X^{tus} inter latrones cruci affixus. Hierusalem a tergo.—*In agata d'Alemagna di fondo rosso incarnato;* scultura *che rosseggia. Cinta d'oro.*

---

* That gems once in the Collection are not there now is curiously illustrated by the absence from the Blenheim cases of the front-face Roman portrait on a sard of perhaps a Cæsar, with the inscription ΑΕΛΙΟC, Vol. ii. No. xxxi. of the "Marlborough Gems"; a gem which must have found its way into the Payne Knight Collection, with which it was bequeathed to the British Museum.

† While this Introduction was passing through the press, the Duke of Marlborough has found at Blenheim some of the very gems here alluded to.

INTRODUCTION.

Theca E. 5. Capita adversa sanctorum Petri et Pauli, hasta cum crucis signo interposita, opus sane perantiquum quod que eximium artificem seculi tertii sapit.—*In sarda questa il suo intaglio prova che nel secolo d'ella primitiva chiesa, come parlamo i novatori, quando accordano, che vigeva la vera dotrina Apostolica, valera l'uso delle Imagini sacre.* 2.

„ E. 24. Mutius Scævola dextram flammis intendit.—*In agata varia.*

The gems brought together by Lord Bessborough at the time the Duke of Marlborough acquired them, had grown into a collection of some importance, not only in consequence of the judicious selections by which they had been increased, but notably by two considerable purchases. By one of these his Lordship added to his Cabinet forty-five gems, the property of Philip Dormer, fourth Earl of Stanhope; and by the other purchase, on the occasion of the sale by auction of the collection of Medina, a Jew, at Leghorn, he acquired forty-seven more; and some of these must have been among the choicest in the Medina Cabinet. That collection as a whole, indeed, had a bad repute for containing many of the fabrications so rife in Italy at that time; but the selection made by or on behalf of Lord Bessborough, while containing such gems as the fabricated Agrippina (No. 417), comprised besides, several admirable and authentic pieces. Among these may be instanced the interesting but mutilated statuette representing Marciana in apotheosis (No. 457); and to this part of the collection of Lord Bessborough belonged the gem (No. 316) once held worthy of passing as a gift from an emperor to a pope. Here also is seen the beautiful Muse in bust (No. 70), corrupted, however, by the false lettering ΣΑΦ; no doubt added at Leghorn to enhance its value.

Among the gems acquired from Lord Chesterfield was the famous intaglio (No. 270), the dog star Sirius, deeply cut into a splendid garnet, and taking the highest rank for its execution and finish among the gems of any age. The taste of this accomplished nobleman is also well illustrated in the interesting portraits that adorned his small cabinet; such as the fine little intaglio representing Marcus Junius Brutus (No. 375), of which No. 376 is probably a copy by Natter's hand; the Sabina (No. 454); the Antoninus Pius (No 462); and the head of Caracalla (No. 485), engraved on a fine sapphire, and interesting as showing the mastery of the engraver at that period over so stubborn a material; nor should the beautiful little ring (No. 551) be omitted as an exquisite example among many of the goldsmith's art.

The acquisition of these two important additions nearly doubled the number of gems that composed Lord Bessborough's Cabinet. Including them, it now numbered two hundred pieces, and was catalogued in French by Laurent Natter, the famous gem engraver, and published in the year 1761. The gems as described in Natter's Catalogue have, with the exception of four, been identified, and references are given to his descriptions under the different gems in this volume. Without doubt, his Lordship had been helped in his acquisitions by the use of Natter's professional opportunities, and had been guided in his selections by the great engraver's excellent taste and intimate acquaintance with the technical details of his art. Moreover, some few of the gems (for instance those numbered in this Catalogue 376, 498) in the part of the collection formed by Lord Bessborough himself, savour not a little of the treatment of that master-hand; and though Natter is in his Catalogue silent as to the sources of such gems, one may sometimes "read between the lines" of his descriptions, and without much chance of error attribute the workmanship to his wheel. That Natter was himself no critical judge of the dates or styles of antique gems is obvious to any one who studies his otherwise interesting "Traité de la Méthode de Graver en Pierres fines;" or who reads his Catalogue of the Bessborough Cabinet by the side of the gems he describes in it: that he frequently copied antiques for practice and for profit is clear also from that work and from the necessities of his occupation. The only question is whether he sold his own works, whether copies or originals, as antiques to his patrons, or whether he was content with the smaller prices they might fetch as the acknowledged productions of his wheel. His silence as to their authorship must not be too readily accepted as condemnatory of him. No one could attribute the imperial heads (No. 498, 1 to 40) under the circumstances to any hand but his; for he speaks of the care with which the choice of the stones had been made, even while he does not assert himself to be their author; indeed, the Duke himself alludes to them as Natter's. It might remove the doubts that have been thrown over gems attributed to him if one could answer the above question in Natter's favour; but it is not easy to do so.

As evidencing the high character and value of many of the gems collected by Lord Bessborough himself, we may instance the great Medusa phalera (No. 100), one of the grandest works on such a hard material as chalcedony in the world; or the deeply cut bust of Pallas

INTRODUCTION. xv

(No. 81), on amethyst, a gem which carries an inscription and possesses a pedigree lacking only one link to make it singularly authentic, and which, if that link could be supplied, would place it with certainty on the first line among gems conspicuous for their archæological interest. Indeed, one should more correctly say that it occupies this place now; and if its rightful claim to that place is to be challenged, it must be by some one who can produce the original by Eutyches, from which so fine an intaglio as this has, as alleged, been taken. The noble intaglio of Jupiter Serapis (No. 5), cut in a large amethyst pebble; the vast Nicolo (No. 256), with its strange African engraving; the Apollo mourning Coronis (No. 60); the Athlete (No. 621), on a paste that has passed under so many names as a stone, and even deceived the knowing eye of Natter; these, too, are illustrations of the skill and judgment with which the Earl of Bessborough—or, rather, perhaps, we should say the Viscount Duncannon, for it was under this his title of courtesy, through his earlier manhood that he was best known to the gem amateur—was guided in his selections for his Cabinet.

If we abstract from the Blenheim Collection as it now stands the gems of the Arundelian and Bessborough Cabinets, we shall find remaining a still noble collection of gems, amounting in number to about the half, and enriched by many splendid pieces, as remarkable in material as they are beautiful or interesting as works of art. This is the portion of the Blenheim Collection that was formed by the third Duke. Foremost among these gems stands the great sardonyx (No. 482); one which will ever rank as one of the most important cameos known, as well on account of the magnitude as of the beautiful character and even deposit of the layers of sard that form the stone.

The uncertainty regarding the Imperial personages it represents, and the date under the Roman Empire at which it was cut, somewhat diminish the interest that should attach to its design, which, moreover, is not of fine execution; but, even apart from the design, the sardonyx alone would possess a considerable value. Then, also, the Augustus already alluded to (No. 390), is a cameo of rare interest and beauty.

Among the intaglios in his Grace's Collection notice may in particular be drawn to the following: the Hermes (No. 165), a noble Greek work; *

---

* It is a very remarkable circumstance that this noble gem was not among the "century" of gems selected by the third Duke for illustration in his work. Worlidge figured it as an Apollo! but Raspe correctly describes the design while he calls the stone a "beryll," "with a "bezle" (No. 2375). He also the Holderness Hermes (No. 167), which, with its inscription of the name ΔΙΟCΚΟΥΡΙΔΟΥ, has, at least, an irreproachable pedigree: the extraordinary but puzzling gem, the green jasper Isis (No. 46); the famous Hercules, with the name ΑΔΜΩΝ (No. 296); the exquisite fragment of Augustus, in the character of Hermes (No. 387); and the Julia of ΝΙΚΑΝΔΡΟΣ, on a transcendent sard (No. 447). These are beautiful specimens of the antique engravers' work, and of modern works by Pichler and Marchant there are several; among which, indeed, must especially be noticed that magnificent work of Marchant, the Return of Alcestis from the Shades, engraved, by command from the Duke of Saxony, as a present to the third Duke, in return for a copy of the two noble volumes in which a hundred of the gems in this cabinet were so splendidly illustrated.

These two folio volumes were produced in the years 1780—1791. Each volume contained copper-plate engravings of fifty gems selected from the collection, with descriptions in Latin and in French: those in the first volume being written in Latin by Mr. James Bryant, and in French by M. P. H. Maty; those in the second volume being written by Mr. W. Cole, and translated into French by M. Dutens. The engravings were done by Bartolozzi, from drawings made by Cipriani from the gems.

A reprint of the work from the old plates, with an introduction more remarkable for its style than for its learning, by the late Mr. Vaughan Thomas, was brought out by the late Duke of Marlborough: but Bartolozzi's fine engravings had lost something of their delicacy and sharpness.

It would be difficult now to trace the history of many of the gems collected by the third Duke, or even to find through what channels he obtained them. In the acquisition of many of the pictures at Blenheim he was aided by Mr. John Udney, for whom the influence of the Duke with Lord Halifax procured the appointment to the British Consulship at Venice, about the year 1761. Through him, also, he was in communication with Count Zanetti and other Italians, who profited by the contemporary fashion of gem collecting. It was in this

describes two copies, one on "beryll," and one on "cornelian," by Burch senior, both in the Duke's Collection. Raspe implies by "beryll" a fine sard; but probably he has been in error as to the latter "beryll," which must be the amethyst No. 166 in this Collection. The cornelian copy may be that figured by Spilsbury (1781-85) as a gem belonging to the Hon. C. Greville, to whom the Duke may have parted with it, as it is not now among the gems of the Collection.

way that the Duke acquired for £600 four gems, the Sabina (No. 455), the Antinous (No. 501), the so-called "Phocion" (No. 538), and the Horatius Cocles (No. 596). With Marchant, some twenty years later, he was in correspondence, sometimes for the purchase of works by Marchant's own hand, sometimes for the acquisition of gems through his agency. This admirable artist appears, so far as can be judged by two or three of his letters, to have been a person of character and of discrimination; and through him his Grace seems to have acquired the beautiful fragment of the large intaglio of Augustus as Mercury (No. 387), a gem with enough of the Greek touch in its treatment to justify at once Marchant's description of it as a Greek work of importance from its magnitude, and the price paid for it, 23 guineas, a sum contrasting favourably with those paid to Zanetti.

The following gems belonged to one collection, but of the name of the owner and the date of its purchase no record remains. The Isis and Horus (No. 45), bought for 10 guineas; the Medusa (No. 99), for 40 guineas; Bacchante's Head (probably that numbered 197), for 70 guineas; the Horatii (No. 609), for 30 guineas; and the fine cameo of a Lion seizing a Bull (No. 716), for 50 guineas. These prices are interesting as examples of the sums paid towards the end of the last century for gems.

From another collection, apparently the property of a French gentleman, the Duke selected the following:—The Isis on garnet (No. 44); the Venus (No. 135); the little cameo (No. 159), with its exquisite mounting, which is a marvel of the jeweller's work of the rarest and most delicate kind; Mercury carrying the Infant Bacchus (No. 169); two gems representing Hercules (No. 295 and No. 300); the portrait of Mary Queen of Scots (No. 589); the Discobolus (No. 623); the Elephant trampling a Fish (No. 705); and the Lion's Head in cat's-eye (No. 717). The sources of a few other gems purchased by the Duke are noticed under their several descriptions; and if documents at Blenheim are silent as to the channels through which his Grace procured some three hundred of the gems in his collection, the purchases above recorded will suffice to prove that he had agents and correspondents in many of the important centres of European commerce and luxury.

A collection so famous as that brought together by the third Duke of Marlborough requires some further notice than a merely historical sketch of its component parts, or the enumeration of a few of its more notable examples of the gem-engraver's art. One would wish, in short, to offer, if not a critical analysis, at least something of a general survey of its contents, such as might serve to determine its position as a collection in respect to the subject it illustrates. And in attempting such a survey we have to bear in mind that a private collection of this kind is not to be judged only by the somewhat narrow standard of archæological criticism. We must, at least, first ask with what purpose it was formed.

The gems in the great public collections of Europe have been brought together with the especial object of illustrating the art and the life of times long past, by means of a class of monuments at once the most varied in their character and the most imperishable in their material. The private gem collector, on the other hand, while appreciating and striving to obtain as perfect examples of this kind as may lie in his power, rarely excludes from association with these antique works the beautiful productions of the Italian Renaissance or of the artists of the last century. And so for a gem to be beautiful is generally a sufficient passport for it into such a private collection, while the interest attaching to the subject, or the stone, or the workmanship, of an antique gem is enough to give it admittance even though it lack the charm of beauty. From a collection so formed, the fastidious archæologist of our critical age would sift and sever the ancient wheat from what in his eyes is but as a mushroom growth of modern tares, and would pass with a cold indifference over the chased and enamelled works of the goldsmith's art in which so many of the Marlborough gems are mounted, and which give them so great a charm for the more comprehensive taste. To form a collection thus representative of all forms of classically treated subjects on gems, and of the best ornamentation they can receive at the hands of the goldsmith, was certainly the purpose which Lord Arundel above two hundred years ago, and which the Duke of Marlborough and other noble collectors among his contemporaries in England during the last century, set before them. These collections, indeed, generally purported to be exclusively classical. Even Natter, who evidently had no more critical knowledge of ancient art than those who employed him or bought his works, while describing the Bessborough Collection, as though to justify the presence in it of a portrait of Oliver Cromwell, speaks of that gem as treated *à l'antique*. No doubt the fine portraits by Jacopo de Trezzo and other masters of the cinque-cento time, were admitted into the Marlborough Collection on similar grounds: on the other hand, several sacred subjects, or subjects that had been so interpreted among the Arundelian Gems, were excluded from his Collection by the Duke of Marlborough; for they are no longer to be found there.

INTRODUCTION.   xix

On reviewing the Blenheim Gems as a whole, one certainly is at first disposed to feel disappointment at the comparatively few examples they afford of very fine and beautiful specimens of the precious and semi-precious materials employed by the gem engraver. On the other hand, as we shall presently show in some detail, there are some very splendid specimens of these materials: but it is also to be observed— and we may appeal herein to the experience of any student of gems —that in general the archæological value of a collection is in an inverse ratio to its wealth in large and beautiful stones. Indeed, where we have two gems similarly treated, and the question arises which is the antique and which the modern imitation, the palm will usually be found awarded to that which is cut on the less beautiful material.

Roughly speaking (for an exact statement is, of course, impossible), the Marlborough Collection may be held to contain about four antique gems to every three of Renaissance and modern age: while of the latter epochs the modern gems slightly preponderate.

From the classical character of the tastes of the times when the different parts of the Collection were formed, we should hardly expect to find in it examples of the cylinders and stamps that for the fifteen hundred years ranging from the dawn of history to the days of Darius Hystaspis, were used by the inhabitants of Mesopotamia and Persia. These interesting monuments of the art of engraving on hard stones, through ages of which scarcely any other arts have survived, have only of late years come to light in any numbers; and though a few were long known to exist in the different European collections, neither the Arundel nor the other parts of the Marlborough Collection contained any of them. Nor, transporting our inquiry from the arts of Asiatic to those of European cities, shall we find in the Marlborough gem cases any of the ruder efforts of an infant art to engrave the Scarabæi used by the Etruscan people from the time of their appearance on the stage of history in Italy. Nor even of the finer productions of Etruscan art should we expect examples in a collection formed at a time when Etruscan tombs were still unransacked. For somewhat similar reasons not only the Scarabæi of Egypt, but those wrought with gem subjects by Phœnician engravers are also absent: for Tharros had as yet been undisturbed. We shall, moreover, look in vain for gems of the archaic period of Hellenic art, a period, however, from which more gems survive than from the period of its perfection, the age of Pericles. That Greek art in its earlier forms should be represented by so exceedingly small a number of gems in the Marlborough Cabinet, may be due chiefly to this scarcity; but partly also to the tastes of the time, which seem to have regarded with more favour the freer and more flowing lines of the styles of the later Greek, the Roman, and modern arts, than it did the severe and carefully, almost cautiously laboured, yet somewhat grotesque, outlines of archaic works. Of the less grotesque and finely finished character, especially as regards the limbs and extremities, which distinguished the earlier Greek from the Etruscan style even in its best time, we may perhaps cite the Horse and Youth (No. 624) as a somewhat late example; it is a beautiful gem, and exhibits well the fine shallow engraving that characterises the earliest as well as the best periods of Greek art.

A short digression may not be out of place here for the purpose of glancing at one or two archæological questions suggested by a review of a collection like the one on which we are engaged. One such question arises out of the rarity of gems belonging to the period of finest art in Greece; while the pre-Phidiac and post-Macedonian periods are, comparatively speaking, richly represented in the gem collections of Europe. It may certainly have been that, in the days when Pericles guided the policy, and Phidias the arts, of Athens, only a wealthy or fastidious few may have worn gems; and that the absence of rings from the fingers of even those graceful horsemen on the frieze of the Parthenon, betokens the more usual custom of that time.

In Solon's age, a century and a half earlier, the inviolability of the signet was secured by a law against the reproduction by the seal-engraver of a signet he had sold. It is not likely that the rings of that age, and the devices on them, were alike always worked in metal: that they usually were so in the Greek world, is, however, probable. On the other hand, the archaic-looking gems which we meet with, cut on sards and tricoloured agates, and, at times, on harder and rarer materials, must, one would suppose, have belonged to the Greek rings of those three half centuries. Scarabæi, with such work on them, have—some two or three of them only—been found on Hellenic soil; and scarabœid-formed gems so found, carrying both early and somewhat later works, are not so exceptionally rare. So that we must suppose that the σφραγίς was not always worn as a ring stone. But most of the Greek gems of this archaic sort, including many with the engrailed or beaded border, are found on oval stones, shaped to be worn in rings. It is difficult to believe, then, that, during the age of Pericles, rings of some sort were not more or less habitually worn in Athens; and if worn, then, also, we can hardly suppose that they would not have had

INTRODUCTION.

their devices, in at least the case of the rich and luxurious, cut on gem stones. We know furthermore from Plato, that at least soon after the death of Pericles, Athenian gentlemen crowded their fingers with jewelled rings. Whether the stones, set in these rings, bore devices, may be questioned; but it is eminently improbable that among them there were not many enriched by the labour of the gem-engraver. Where then are these gems now? Have we still new treasures to discover in some as yet unviolated necropolis?

It is improbable; and our conclusion is, that gems engraved on stones must either have been rarer during the Phidiac and immediately post-Phidiac time than in the centuries before or after, or, that these gem stones have been lost to us by some special cause. Indeed, we have pastes enough remaining to our time made from fine Greek gems of the class we are discussing, to prove that, in some shape or other, such gems, either on stone or metal, existed in some numbers.

If they had been engraved on precious metal we need not go far to explain their destruction; but for such as were engraved on stone we must look again perhaps to the preciousness of the material for our explanation. An artist of a later age, for instance a Syracusan gem-engraver in the reign of Hiero II., might possibly have looked on some fine stone adorned with the shallow scooped work, the stately design and the correct modelling of the severer Greek time as a valuable prize; though not so much from the work it carried as from its material, for it would have afforded him a well selected stone on which he could cut some design more in harmony with the deep relief and elaborate detail prized in his own age and country, where wealth, and that natural development of Arts from the severe into the voluptuous, must have begun to sap the sentiment which made Magna Græcia imitate the Helladic cities in the severity of the types employed on their coinages.

But if we are thus to offer one possible explanation for the disappearance of such few gems as we assume must have belonged to the greatest age of Art, we may perhaps be justified in asking whether the Art of Greece really extended, in its perfection, beyond the soil of a few Helladic States. In those States the architecture and adornment of temples probably absorbed nearly the whole artistic energy and genius of the people, and the men who copied the statues of a Phidias or a Polycletus for signets would, from this cause no less than because the demand would only arise when the statues had become famous, naturally be the gem-engravers of a subsequent time; a time when the schools of Praxiteles and Scopas, on the one hand, or that of Lysippus on the other, were rapidly bringing new artistic ideals into vogue. And it is, moreover, not a little probable that a certain affectation of the archaic may have lingered in the gem-engraver's art, as it did so long in some cases with the kindred art of the die-sinker, and that thus many of the finer gems that we should otherwise place in the previous centuries may really have to be ascribed to these.

So, it may be, it happens that we meet occasionally even on scarabæi, as also on the kind of gems usually considered to be early Greek, subjects curiously resembling both in design and treatment those which belong to the coinages of such cities as Corinth, Heraclea, Tarentum, or Naxos. But however we seek to meet the great difficulty presented by the comparative blank as regards Phidiac gems in our collections, we feel that we are really baffled in our attempts to explain it, and we are forced to acknowledge that it is only one out of a thousand proofs of the very fragmentary nature of our knowledge about the daily life of antiquity, in any time or country.

The broad features and outlines of some ancient scene we can with more or less of verisimilitude depict; but how often have we not to call on our imagination to fill up the details, or to represent, with the living reality of colour, the men and women, the buildings—all, indeed, save earth and sky—when we would for a moment climb with ancient Greeks the Acropolis of Athens, or mingle in the throng of the Roman Forum!

The rare and noble portrait-heads of Macedonian, Ptolemaic, and other Greek sovereigns, from the days of Alexander to those of Mithridates, show us the various styles of work and degrees of finish attained by the gem-engravers of that period of two centuries. They are generally, however, rather vigorous than minutely laboured in their finish; in fact, just redeemed from being hard in treatment by their fine modelling: and we are strongly disposed to attribute to the latter part of this period, and to the subsequent pre-Augustan and Augustan age the more elaborately finished and delicate works of the Greek gem-engraver. Indeed, the fine sards from India, and the adamantine materials for engraving on them, must at that time have begun to be common, and to improve the technique of the art. The bold but elaborate treatment of Syracusan coins, and of some of those of Magna Græcia, seems to suggest a parallelism with the deeply cut intaglios that we are constrained by their very perfection of artistic design and technical treatment to place in the period when the art was purely Greek; and this deep-engraving seems to have become a Roman taste, and to have been adopted by some of the Greco-Roman gem-cutters of the Augustan and of after times.

INTRODUCTION.   xxiii

But who were these engravers of Greek and Roman signets? and whence did they draw the subjects for their designs? A skilled eye can without much hesitation recognise in the design of a gem the source whence the artist drew it, whether a statue, a bas-relief, or a mural fresco; and undoubtedly all of these forms of art suggested such designs. Many of the Etruscan and finer archaic works present certainly the characteristics of the last of these forms of art; a form to which we know the inhabitants of Tuscany and Rome to have been as partial in very early days as they continued to be until the age of Raphael. Both in subject and treatment these pictorial gems recall to mind the representations of heroic myths, handed down to us on Greek vases of the period just bordering on the Phidiac age. The gems of the later Greek style, on the other hand, frequently consist of individual divinities in the sculpturesque attitudes characteristic of the bronze or marble statues that drew the delight and reverence of Greeks. But it is contrary to the genius of the two arts to suppose that the sculptor and the sculptor were one and the same person, that the γλυφή of the one and the γλάφυ, if we may so use the word, of the other, were the work of a single hand. It is a much more natural supposition that if the gem-engraver's art was not entirely distinct, its affinities with the art of the die-sinker would tend to make the master-designer, whose artist hand cut the pattern pieces of a noble Greek coinage, also the engraver of the choicest gems, and the artizans who repeated the coin-dies would, in this case, be his natural disciples in either art. The treatment of a design on a coin was indeed generally somewhat stiffer and harder than on the gem, and the variety of subjects was more restricted. The first of these results was naturally due to the nature of the material and the mode of employing it; the second arose, of course, as in the case of vases, from the greater variety of individual tastes, the subjects being much circumscribed in the case of the coin by the special character of the associations that were hallowed in a city or a nation.

But notwithstanding these differences in the two arts, there remained a great similarity in the subjects and in the motive of each of them, a similarity that certainly seems to point to the mints of Grecian cities as the probable schools from which the gem-engraver and the master die-sinker would alike have emerged. In the Roman Imperial age, it is hard to resist the conclusion, that the same hand must have been master of both arts.

Yet here again we can only urge probability and the sort of argument that is drawn from analogy to support this view. But whatever uncertainty and hesitation may prevent our fully and satisfactorily answering the questions we have raised, we may feel very sure that many a myth—including some that have been in other forms lost to us—is handed down to our days on the imperishable sard and in scarcely any other tangible form; and that of many a master-piece of the Grecian Sculptor we have the general form and air perpetuated on gems, that have been lost in every other shape; and on this too we may assuredly rely, that if we could but assemble in one collection the still extant gem-signets of the different ages and families of man from the days of Urukh to those of the latest Sassanian kings, we should have a more complete representation of the objects that stirred the minds and ruled the hearts of men through all those many ages and changes of circumstance, than would be afforded by any other single form of their arts—indeed we may perhaps with justice say, than by all the other forms of these that remain to us combined.

It is, of course, with more or less of conjecture, guided by a somewhat halting experience, that we attempt to discriminate between the gems of the post-Phidiac Greek schools, or even hazard an opinion regarding the relative date of those belonging to the later Greek and early Imperial Roman epochs. The works of Praxiteles and of the Lysippan school indubitably formed subjects for the gem-engraver, and they must have been copied, though particular subjects would of course have been in fashion in different times and places, during the whole of the later Greek and Greco-Roman periods. But not less indubitably must the gem carry on its face now the evidence of the hand that worked it long ago, if only our eyes be enough skilled in the sort of criticism that can discern the differences of *technique* and treatment. How hard this is, even with all the wealth of modern museums in statues, bronzes, coins, and friezes, the accomplished archæologist and most scholarlike critic, perhaps the most deeply feels. That the student of a single subject like gem engraving—though, indeed, such a subject cannot be altogether singly studied—should feel this difficulty while hazarding opinions regarding the age of the different gems he describes, is not to be wondered at. But it seemed, nevertheless, better to face this difficulty, and in the subjoined Catalogue to venture to assign to the different works what seemed to its author their probable dates, than, from the fear that some might be erroneous, to leave the finest works in the collection with a bare and colourless description, unlinked by any suggestion with either epoch in the history of Art. Whether that grand ruin, the polished-out Apollo (No. 50), or that numbered 51 in this Catalogue, both from the Arundelian Collection, one at least of

INTRODUCTION. xxv

which seems to reflect the style of the Apollo of Miletus, were wrought in the later Æginetan or the Phidiac, or even in a still later age; whether, again, the grand figure of Hermes (No. 165) is a work of near the age of Lysippus or a copy by a great Greek hand in the later Greek or early Greco-Roman period from a statue belonging to the Lysippan school, one has really too little data—at least, our experience is not enough—to say with any confidence. But that in these gems we are looking on types familiar to the men who lived in those great epochs of noble art, types which we see refracted, as it were, down to our days through the sards in which native Greek hands at some time during the golden age had imaged them, is beyond doubt. Nor can we hesitate in giving a Greek, though a less early Greek date, to the workmanship, and perhaps to the design, of the Satyr rejoicing in the grape (No. 215), on a lovely hyacinth; or to the Muse (No. 70), or the Mourning Apollo (No. 60).

When we have reached the Augustan age the numbers of good gems in the Collection thicken on us; and we may almost cease to particularise among them, or at least to do so further than will have been done in other parts of this Introduction. In fact, it is to the centuries between the reign of Augustus and the end of the Antonine period, that we have to refer the major part of the gems in this as in most other fairly selected collections of gems. And among these the gems are most numerous and conspicuous that were worked about the period of the reign of Hadrian, during the marked revival in that reign of the arts that had receded so far in the previous reigns from the perfection of the Augustan age.

To this time belongs of course that marvellously fine Antinous on a black sard, that has been so often copied in the last century (No. 500 in this Catalogue); and to this age, too, must be referred several of the polychrome cameos cut in the differently coloured layers of sardonyx in that reign coming into vogue, the material of which was, perhaps, then supplied in larger and choicer specimens by the extending commerce with the East. Possibly to this age is to be assigned that marvel of art, the great chalcedony phalera (No. 100), though it is difficult to believe that it is not a work of an earlier and a nobler period in the history of Art.

Of the classes of gems, Egyptian in their subjects, but belonging in date to the Ptolemaic and Romano-Egyptian periods, there are a few examples in the Blenheim Collection. The portrait (No. 364) of Demetrius Philopator, though not Egyptian, is of Ptolemaic date and Greek workmanship; and probably the splendid cameo (No. 366) of an

d

Egyptian queen, may claim Greco-Ptolemaic date and origin. So, too, may the cameo on lapis lazuli (No. 319) of two profile busts, probably royal, as Hercules and Iole. The beautiful hyacinthine garnet, with a head of Isis (No. 43), is Romano-Egyptian, if it be not even Ptolemaic; while the gems, Nos. 44 and 46, belong to the later of these periods. On pages 49 and 50 will be found the description of five gems, also of this later age. The heads of Serapis, so common under the Roman Empire, were certainly engraved in other parts of the Empire besides Egypt. Of the Mithraic subjects, which the infiltration of the Persian religious system into the Empire had called into existence, there are two examples, described in page 49. Nor are the rudely worked gnostic gems unrepresented here; gems with enigmatical subjects, such as were the talismans and amulets of Basileides, which, to judge from their numbers, must have sprung up, a plentiful crop, from the Alexandrian hotbed of the Gnosis, in the second century. The examples in this Collection are described on page 51. Of the works of the Lower Empire after Severus Alexander, a period when gem engraving in Rome had become well-nigh barbarous, we should not expect to find examples in this Collection. Indeed there are not, perhaps, half a dozen Roman gems in it of later date than the reign of Elagabalus, even if we include some of the memorial rings and souvenirs described on page 106 of this Catalogue. Nor, again, of the very numerous gems remaining to our time from the days of the Persian Empire under the Sassanian sovereigns—so conspicuous for the exquisite stones on which their designs are engraved, and for the coarse wheel-wrought character of the designs themselves—were any considered worthy of a place in the Blenheim Collection; probably, indeed, its noble collector was not acquainted with them at all. Even Byzantine gems are unrepresented in it. These gems are absent, no doubt, for the reason that the art was ceasing to be "classical," as well in subjects as in treatment.

But after the long sleep of the gem-engraver's, as of other classical forms of Art, through those active centuries that we call the Dark Ages, while the civilization and polities of modern Europe were fermenting out from the great turmoil that attended, and partly caused, the decadence of the divided Empire, came that age of the Renaissance, the era of the Medicis.

Of the re-awakened arts of that era gem engraving was one, and it of course reflected the characters of the rest. Without entering on the history of its growth and progress, we may point to a few of the finer examples of the period in the great Collection under our review.

INTRODUCTION. xxvii

The spinel or ruby signet of Charles cinq of France (No. 583), and the exquisite and famous cameo, the Nuptials of Cupid and Psyche, have already been alluded to when speaking of the Arundel Collection. The latter illustrates by the charm of its drawing, the perfection of its execution, its very errors in classical detail, and in the relation which the design bears to the form and size of the surface it adorns, all the characteristics of the best time of the Renaissance.

Among the many cameos and portraits of that period, none can surpass the grand head (No. 538), probably representing some personage contemporary with the famous artist Alessandro il Greco who engraved it. The portraiture of that period of art is further represented in the cameo likenesses of the Emperor Charles V., of Philip II. (probably by Jacopo de Trezzo), of Henri IV., and of Cardinal Mazarin.

Among the modern gems, which are especially numerous in the portion of the collection formed by the third Duke himself, are to be found works by Sirletti (the Laocoon, on amethyst, No. 349, is one), by Natter, by Pichler, by Burch, and by Marchant, who aided his Grace in the purchase of some of his finest and most authentically antique gems while resident in Rome.

This sketch would be incomplete without some notice of the materials to the durability of which we owe the preservation, and to the beauty of which is due so much of the charm of a collection of gems. The stones employed by the gem-engraver in ancient times differ but little from those in use for the purpose in the Renaissance and modern ages. The commonest material in each age has been chalcedony in one or other of its numerous and varied forms. Next to chalcedony come the garnets, the amethyst, lapis lazuli, the beryl, the sapphire, the peridot, the emerald; while some late gems, chiefly amulets, engraved with gnostic and astrological subjects, are met with on hæmatite and occasionally on magnetite, the mineral forms of two of the oxides of iron. With the exception of the last two, these stones engraved with antique work occur with a frequency represented by the order in which we have recounted them.

But the chalcedonic minerals offer the most coveted materials to the gem-engraver, who prizes their fine grain,—or rather absence of grain and crystalline cleavage—their toughness, and their hardness, which is such as to yield most readily to the materials (diamond and emery dust) wherewith he charges his wheel; while on the other hand they are able to resist the abrasion of ordinary materials, and the more subtle erosion of Time. These stones also are all susceptible of an excellent polish, and are many of them endowed with the gift of beautiful colour. Hence to one stone of any other material we find perhaps ten composed of some form of chalcedony. Chalcedony is composed of silica in a form devoid of visible crystallisation, while quartz is that earth completely crystallised. The amethyst and the citrine are violet and yellow forms of quartz; the former was the amethystus (ἀμέθυστος) of antiquity; the latter is probably one of the stones known to Pliny under the Greek term chrysolithus.

In passing, attention may be called to one or two of the beautiful amethysts in this Collection. As specimens of large size and of the streaked and paler colours, very usual in the antique ateliers, we may mention the great pebble (No. 5) with the Serapis intaglio, and the famous Pallas of Eutyches (No. 81), the stone of which bears a strong indirect testimony to the genuineness of the work, for a modern forger would have chosen an amethyst of at least a richer hue. Quartz, crystallus (κρύσταλλος), seldom occurs with antique work upon it: a specimen of it, however, penetrated by fibres of rutile, a rare material for a gem, is here seen with a figure of the Sun God (No. 266).

We reserve the term chalcedony for the comparatively colourless varieties of the mineral; they generally have a pale smoky, yellowish or bluish hue. When coloured with any of the tints of red and yellow which the oxide of iron imparts to it, it becomes the sard (σάρδιον, sarda), so called from this word meaning yellow in Persian, not from the town of Sardis, Pliny's etymology; the pale rich yellow kind, clear yellow when looked through, and pale dull orange or brownish yellow when looked at, is the golden sard; the yellow sard being the name for the less translucent specimens which lack the brightness of the former and have a yellower or more orange tint when looked at. The golden sard was the favourite stone of the Greek artist, who doubtless meant the work he engraved on it to be seen as a transparency. The yellow sard only occasionally carries antique work.

The sardine-stone or sardine, the *sardoine* of the French, is a dark red translucent, but sometimes very transparent, sard, the aspect of which is almost black; its fine colour being only seen when it is looked through. It often carries noble work of the late Greek, and early Imperial Roman periods; but still oftener the works of the cinque-cento and modern artists.

The "hyacinthine" sard is the term applied to a rich and glorious variety of this stone which possesses the orange-red tint, with almost the transparency of the kind of garnet termed in France "hyacinthe la belle." To these clear and beautiful kinds of sard, the writers of the last century gave the name of beryl, a term that has introduced many a case of confusion into the descriptions of gems in that century, such as the account Raspe gives of the famous Hermes (No. 165) in this Collection, which he states to be engraved on a beryl.

The duller transparent red kinds of sardine are the blood sard; and there are varieties of the sard of every tone of red, orange and brown, from an opaque black sard on the one hand, to the pale golden kind on the other. And the sard passes by gradual steps into the cornelian, a stone from which it is, however, mineralogically distinguishable. Thus the true sard presents in its fracture a dull, hackly aspect, due probably to a microscopically-crystalline structure, not inconsistent with its very homogeneous substance, and absence of grain. It is also tougher and much harder than the cornelian, which is readily chipped, and exhibits a smooth glistening surface of fracture. The cornelian probably contains more of the opaline silica, the sard and the other chalcedonies possessing what has been termed a crypto-crystalline character, and therefore being more nearly of the nature of quartz.

In considering the other coloured varieties of chalcedony, we may next pass to those that are green. They are known by the term Plasma (a corruption, it is said, of Prasina). They present almost every tint and hue of green, yellow-green, and bluish-green, and sometimes almost rival the emerald in the beauty of the colour transmitted through them, though in translucency and lustre they can never compete with that splendid stone. Their colouring matter is usually iron, but sometimes, also, it is the chromium which gives its colour to the emerald. The chalcedony tinted by nickel, the chrysoprase of mineralogy, if it ever occurs with antique work, which is extremely doubtful, certainly only does so very rarely. It is rare, indeed, to meet with gems on plasma, the transparency and homogeneity of which are not spoilt by flaws and flecks throughout their substance. The jaspis of the Romans probably included some of the less translucent varieties. 'Viret et sæpe trahicet iaspis, etiam victa multis antiquitatis gloriam retinens," is Pliny's introduction to the species of jaspis. Undoubtedly the "antiquitatis gloria" must allude to the habitual use of the green jasper, for gems and for ornaments, by the Egyptians and Phœnicians of the eld. They, however, very rarely employed the translucent kinds of stone, through which the green jasper passes into the plasma. The expression "sæpe tralucet" shows that translucency was not the essential characteristic of the jaspis, as advocated by some authors.

INTRODUCTION.

Some of the more transparent and richly tinted varieties of the plasma fell certainly among the species of the smaragdus of Pliny. Probably the ἴασπις of the Greeks included the same varieties of stone as Pliny's "iaspis;" but no Greek work that can certainly be attributed to the better periods of art is known upon any of these materials. A few archaic Greek works are, however, certainly known on a translucent plasma; but the stone came first into general use and fashion during the early Imperial epoch; when good Imperial portraits were engraved on it. A little later it became a very common material for gems, and generally carries work remarkable for the beauty of the drawing and design, but of rather coarse workmanship in the details. These gems probably, if we may judge from the subjects common on them, belong chiefly to the period between Titus and the Antonines. Indeed, the Venus Victrix on the coins of that time is so frequent a subject on the plasma, as to suggest the idea that it may have been worn as a talisman or charm by the gentler sex (see No. 124).

A pale and delicate bluish chalcedony is that known as the sapphirine chalcedony. Heads and figures of Jove are not very uncommon upon it. An amethystine and a rose-tinted variety, the former usually with Asiatic work, are also occasionally met with.

Of the stones that we recognise by the name of jasper, which are chalcedonies charged with a sufficient amount of foreign matter to render them opaque, and which present a beautiful variety and vividness in their colours, none except the black or brownish-black varieties seem to have been employed by the Greeks, though in Roman Imperial times the other varieties came into vogue.

The Egyptians, indeed, as already mentioned, were partial to a dark green jasper owing its colour to the mineral chlorite, and Phœnician scarabæi are usually formed of this stone, some kinds of which are very soft, from their containing an excessive amount of this ingredient, or of the mineral termed "green earth." A pale green jasper, that composing the material of the singular gem in this Collection (No. 40), was also sometimes used by the Egyptians for their inlaid gold *cloisonnée* work; but as materials for gems of a good period of the art, these green varieties of jasper are very rare.

Of the dark green jasper there are two other kinds: the bloodstone is an opaque, and the heliotrope is a translucent variety which, in fact, is a dark plasma; both are characterised by red or sometimes yellow opaque stains or spots. All these stones were employed during the decline of the art in the second century—being favourite stones for astrological and gnostic subjects; the Sun God, with radiate crown and whip in hand, and often in a chariot, being frequently found engraved on them.

The vermilion-coloured jasper—"hæmatitis" of Pliny, and not to be confounded with our hæmatite, which is the native oxide of iron, though this is the colouring matter of the red jasper—is unknown as a gem stone before the Imperial Roman era had set in ; in fact, Greek work on it probably does not exist. A few fine antique gems are known engraved on it, but in the best of them there is a coarseness of manipulation and finish that generally reveals the fact that they were worked by the wheel at the time when it was superseding all the other tools of the engraver. This period was probably about the reign of Trajan. The design on the red jasper is generally more stiff than on the plasma, which seems to have preceded it by some years in the fashions at Rome. The head of Vespasian (No. 441) in this Collection is probably a contemporary work, and a very early example of this material; but when we come to the days of Hadrian, and more particularly of his Antonine successors, the red jasper often carries imperial portraits with the characteristics of the work of those times. The influence of the material on the art it embodies is interestingly exhibited in the red jasper gems. As a material it seems not susceptible of the delicacy of workmanship that the tough and grainless sard so admirably responds to, and which was the first essential in a gem stone with the Greek artist. The lines have, therefore, to be coarser on the jasper ; but, on the other hand, its duller and more earthy lustre befits this coarser work and sets it off well, while, from the brilliant colour of the stone, the effect of none of the work on the red variety is lost. On the green stones, and this is particularly true of the plasmas, the duller hue, or rather, the greater absorption of light and illuminating colours by the stone, prevent the details and modelling of the work on these stones from being well seen, unless by a lens or in strong light; and this has probably been the cause that while the engraver usually drew his outlines with freedom and artistic expression on the plasmas, the work with which the details are put in on them is so often sketchy and almost rude. And if the Greek preferred a transparent stone in general, that his work might be enjoyed as a transparency, the Roman gem-engraver seems to have wrought with a view to the effect of his work when seen directly by reflected light. Probably with both the, so to say, business use of the gem for forming an impression, was considered as of less importance in the artistic point of view than its being an object of admiration as an ornament. In many cases, again, it was neither as a signet nor as an ornament so much as in the character of a talisman that a gem was worn : and for this it was only necessary that a certain subject should be engraved on a particular stone. The silent language of Art had little power to persuade or elevate where superstitions like these of the Orphic school of mystics, had dominated the reason and sealed the senses.

And to this cause, as much as to any other, is due the decline of the gem-engraver's art, even while other and kindred arts had made much less progress towards their eclipse.

The onyx, sardonyx, and banded agate, are forms of agate ; and agate is chalcedonic silica, deposited in successive layers, in general, in the interior of the hollows that occur in trap rocks. The deposits that have thus lined and gradually filled these hollows, must have been formed by an intermittent action, as the outline, and often the colour and other characters, of each are distinct. They seem to have been produced by an infiltration—thus intermittent—of silicious waters into the hollow ; the silica depositing itself over the walls of the cavity, or collecting round some nucleus within it. The result is a solid mass of silica, built up of layers nearly parallel to each other, and following the contortions and angles of the surface of the cavity. A section through such a mass will, therefore, reveal a series of parallel bands or stripes, sometimes angular, and curved, and curiously tortuous, sometimes, however, level and nearly straight, like the stripes of a ribbon. The layers or bands in these stones present different properties. Thus in the same stone some of the layers may have the quality of sard, and like that stone, be somewhat porous; others, again, being colourless or white, and resisting infiltration. The layers of the former kind have, in some cases, been infiltrated by the weak solution of iron salts occurring in the water that has permeated the rock, and have either become subsequently coloured by the iron oxide, through exposure to the air, or needed only the application of heat to develope in them the red or yellow hues of the sard. To such, again, as have not been thus naturally and *throughly* tinted, artificial colour may be imparted by the absorption of colouring solutions of iron or other metals, or of honey, and by a subsequent treatment by sulphuric and other acids, or by heat.

This art has particularly been practised in Germany, near Oberstein, where a more porous and inferior kind of agate is met with. The hills of Malwa have from the earliest days, and those of Uruguay have in quite recent times, supplied the finer kinds, rich in their layers of true sard. The layers of the inferior sorts belong to a variety of chalcedony, more allied to the cornelian than to the sard.

The level and flatly laminated agates may be cut either parallel to or

INTRODUCTION.

transversely to the direction of the strata. The so-called onyxes and sardonyxes of the gem-engraver are the stones produced by the former method: the long, oval-formed, "banded" or "tri-coloured" agates (No. 257 of this Collection), on which so many of the fine Etruscan and later Greek works are engraved, are the transversely cut specimens. The term agate is usually retained for those more irregular varieties of stone in which the layers present angularities in their outlines.

The (achates) agate of Pliny, no doubt, was also applied to the less transparent of these and to the more variegated kinds of jasper; the term onyx among the ancients having been used in different senses at diverse times. Our "banded agate" represents, perhaps, the ὀνύχιον of the Greeks, the more transparent of the fantastic and irregular agates being the onyx of the Romans; though the term seems also to have been used for varieties of the sardonyx, the layers of which were not sard. A sardonyx (σαρδῷος ὄνυξ), however, was certainly a stone in which the strata lay superposed, and in which one layer at least was sard.

Much confusion has been introduced into modern descriptions of gems by the different senses in which the terms onyx and sardonyx have been used. One fashion confines the term onyx to the two-layered stones, and that of sardonyx to those in which more than two layers are superposed, irrespective of their quality.

In the descriptions in the following Catalogue, the term onyx will be used to imply a stone in which chalcedonic layers of various hues and kinds are superposed, provided none of these be of the sard character. Where one of these is sard, the stone will be termed a sardonyx. Practically, the two terms are difficult of very exact discrimination; as, for instance, where the sard-like layers are of inferior or opaque quality; in the last case, the stone passes into a jasper onyx.

But in all ambiguous cases the descriptions given of each stone will render a more exact terminology unnecessary.

The sardonyx has always been the favourite material for cameos. The artists of the Ptolemaic period probably first used its differently coloured layers—at least, of the two-layered stones—in order to impart a contrast to the different surfaces of their designs. The exaggerated use of this artifice in stones with several differently tinted layers belongs to the Roman period; its effect was to produce a strong and conventional, rather than a pleasing, contrast.

The term nicolo—abbreviated from *onyculo*—is applied to a variety, generally two-layered, of the onyx; the base layer being usually an opaque black jasper, sometimes artificially blackened, sometimes also a

xxxiv   INTRODUCTION.

dark sard, while the very thin surface layer is of a pale bluish-white hue, due partly to the white of the upper layer not being pure, and partly to the effect of the black stratum below it being dimly seen through the translucent substance of this thin upper layer. Work of an earlier time than the Augustan age, on the nicolo, is probably not known; but from that time onwards it carries fair but rarely very good work, generally characterised by a certain clumsiness in the drawing, and by inferior character in the treatment. The works on it were done to present a pictorial effect, the thin bluish upper layer being cut through to the dark base layer of the stone; so that the design is seen in black on a bluish-white ground. To give effect to the design—thus, dark on a white ground—a certain exaggeration in outline became necessary; just as, had the white layer been that employed to represent the subject, a more attenuated outline would be found to be required.

The nicolo continued to be a rather favourite stone, so long as gem engraving existed as an art; and among the gems of the Sassanian Dynasty in the Parthian Empire we find mingled with many luminous and lovely sards, and with transcendent garnets, nicolos presenting the finest contrasts in their colours; all these stones carrying the singular and rudely worked subjects which seem to have represented an art inherited from the days of Mesopotamian cylinders and Persian conical stamps, but modified in its *technique* by the introduction of methods, especially the use of a coarse wheel, from the West.

This stone may have been the Ægyptilla of Pliny, "nigrâ radice, cœruleâ facie."

The interesting cameo, No. 4 in this Catalogue, representing the Jupiter Axur, known also on the famous intaglio with the inscription **NEICOY** at St. Petersburg; the Omphale, also in cameo, on the historically interesting *double* nicolo (No. 316), composed of a black stratum between two bluish-white strata, and perforated by the original Indian boring; the huge stone with its strange African representation of the Lybian Astarte (No. 256); may be instanced among the remarkable ancient nicolos in the Marlborough Collection.

Next in importance and frequency to the large family of chalcedonic stones comes the mineralogical group known under the name of garnet, the ἄνθραξ of the Greek, and carbunculus of the Roman writers. Not to complicate the subject by mineralogical details, the garnets used by the gem-engravers may be divided according to their colour. The pure transcendently red varieties, without tints of orange on the one hand, or of violet on the other, when seen by transmitted light, and

INTRODUCTION.

known by various names, such as Bohemian garnet (slightly brownish in its hue), Syriam garnet, so called from Syriam, the capital of Pegu, and pyrope, form for our purpose one division : a second will be made up of the kinds inclining to orange when examined by transmitted light. These orange varieties, when toned with brown, and of the tint of Tavel, or tawny port wine, are the "guarnacino" garnets of the Italians. Those kinds in which the orange tends to an aurora red, are the hyacinthine garnet—the hyacinths of the jewellers. They are identical in colour with, but less lustrous than, the true hyacinth or red jacinth, which is a zircon. Often they exhibit paler and more yellow hues, and are internally seen to be full of striæ and bubble-like impurities : these are the cinnamon stone. They are doubtless one of the kinds of chrysolithus that were admired in Imperial Rome; and fine work of the Imperial age, and sometimes beautifully drawn and modelled Greek art, are met with on them.

The next variety of the garnets—thus classed according to their colours—is the kind which exhibits a violet hue mixed with the red when the stone is seen by transmitted light. They are the Oriental garnets of the jewellers, India furnishing some of the best of them. They are also called the almandine garnets, possibly from the ancient term *alabandici*, as applied to a variety of the carbunculus worked at and exported from Alabanda, in Caria. The modern term carbuncle applies to any kind of garnet that is cut "en cabochon." Fair work on this lovely stone, the almandine, is not rare in the Roman period. There is generally a sort of characteristic roughness and want of polish in the interior of the designs on this stone in ancient times, contrasting curiously with the finer polish, which again corresponds often with a higher quality in the work, on the guarnacino, and hyacinthine, and cinnamon (or essonite) garnets of the epoch of Imperial Rome, or of the late Greek art that existed just before that epoch. The pretty gem (No. 27) representing Neptune, is a fine example of ancient work on this stone. No. 229 is also a beautiful example of Roman work on it. Of the hyacinthine garnet we have examples in Nos. 43 and 330; while No. 123 is a garnet of the quality known as the Syrian or Syriam garnet, with work that seems Roman in date upon it. No. 728 may be another gem also of Roman workmanship, on a similar stone, one worthy of comparison with that in which the famous Sirius (No. 270) is sunk.

Lapis lazuli, the sapphirus ($\sigma\acute{a}\pi\phi\epsilon\iota\rho\sigma s$) of antiquity, is a stone on which Greek and Roman work of every age—unless, perhaps, of the earliest (archaic) Greek time—is met with. Yet, though thus wide in its horizon - to use a geological phrase—it seems never to have been a common material for gems. The Mercury (No. 170) and the Hercules and Iole cameo (No. 319), will serve to illustrate the use of this material at two different periods ; and both are fine examples of the stone.

Among the rarer stones employed by the ancients, of which examples are to be met with in this Collection, the sapphire—the hyacinthus of Roman authors—is the hardest, and is among the scarcest to be met with. The Medusa (No. 98), and the head of Caracalla (No. 485), are remarkable illustrations of the stone, and of the mastery the Roman artists had acquired over its stubborn material. The beryl (beryllus), a less rare stone in antiquity than the sapphire, and, like it, Oriental in one at least of its sources, is well illustrated in the Neptune (No. 25) and the Hippocampus (No. 734), both, it may be observed, marine subjects—a class for which this material was often employed by the ancients.

The Julia Domna (No. 484), the Bacchus (No. 183), and the Gryllus (No. 690), are also excellent and very interesting examples of antique work on the beryl, a stone in which the Blenheim Collection is thus seen to be especially rich.

Of the ruby, the emerald, and the peridot, the Collection contains no antique specimens.

The turquoise is represented by a gem of singular beauty, the Livia and Tiberius cameo (No. 403). Pliny speaks of the callaina as having the hue of the topazius (our peridot), only being opaque. This is exactly the tint and character of this green turquoise—the favourite variety with the Romans. Of the blue variety, no doubt the callais, the little cameo (No. 532) seems to be an authentic antique specimen.

The gems in the Collection have all been marked with numbers, generally in a vermilion colour; and these numbers are those which belong to the following Catalogue.

In this Catalogue, whenever a gem has been identified with one in the collection of Lord Bessborough, as catalogued by Natter, a reference is given to his published catalogue with the number in it of the gem. The gems acquired from the collections of Lord Chesterfield and of Medina, are severally distinguished by the letters C and M, and by numbers also referring to the published catalogue of Natter. Similar references are given to the gems that can be identified with those described in the catalogue of the Arundel Collection, as it stood in Lady Elizabeth Germain's time. The gems of the former of these collections stand at present in three of the cases at Blenheim, marked B I, B II, and B III, sufficiently nearly in the order in which they are

INTRODUCTION. xxxvii

described in Natter's catalogue, to corroborate by their position in the cases any opinion one might, in a few instances, have otherwise given with hesitation, regarding their identification. The Arundelian Gems are mixed up in the remaining cases with those acquired by the third Duke. The greater part of these can be fairly well recognised under the descriptions in the catalogue preserved at the Society of Antiquaries. Some of the gems in that catalogue are certainly no longer in the collection : a few, again, are not described so plainly as to be capable of being identified with certainty, though this does not seem to apply to any of the more important gems. A reference is occasionally made to a catalogue already alluded to—drawn up by the third Duke—which was probably intended ultimately for publication. But in general when no reference is made to the Bessborough or Arundel collections, the gem was one of those collected by the third Duke himself. The descriptions given by His Grace of the Bessborough and Arundel gems are those of Natter's, or of the Arundelian Catalogue, of which he must have possessed a copy; and they are but little altered. Raspe's catalogue of Tassie's casts has also, of course, been among the many works ransacked to trace the history of the gems.

In using the phrase " to the right," or " to the left," as applied to a head or bust, the direction is that of the head on the gem itself as seen by the spectator, not that on the cast from it. The terms "confronted" and "conjoined" are used respectively for faces represented as looking towards each other, or as looking the same way where one is partly eclipsed by the other.

The term "conjugated" will be reserved for cases in which heads are united, as in the Campanian coins of Janus, or as in the caprices and medleys of masks, so common upon gems.

Inscriptions on the intaglios are to be considered as retrograde, unless described as being otherwise. It remains only for the author of this Catalogue to appear for a moment on the scene, to express personal gratitude to many who have helped him with their wider experience and larger learning. But first he has to explain the *raison d'être* of this Catalogue at all.

In 1861, the Archæological Institute formed an exhibition of all the collections of antique gems that could be brought together in London. Her Majesty lent the Royal Collection from the Presence Chamber at Windsor, and the Dukes of Marlborough and Devonshire committed their famous Collections also to the care of the Institute.

The author of this Catalogue had, when living at Oxford, made some study of the knowledge of minerals possessed by the ancients at various periods; and such a rich assortment of the materials used in gem engraving, as that brought together in 1861, seemed to offer a great opportunity for practical research in this subject. But the difficulty of deciding the dates and styles of the work on gems, or even their claims to antiquity, rendered a much more elaborate study of the gems and of their subjects necessary.

The Duke of Marlborough was, at the close of the exhibition, induced to lend his splendid inheritance of gems to the author for his study and for inspection by those who might wish to see the collection in detail.

A catalogue was the first requisite for this study; and a rough catalogue of the gems as they stood was accordingly made, chiefly during a first inspection of them with Mr. King of Trinity College, Cambridge. Mr. King published the result of his inspection in the Archæological Journal of 1862. Under the author's hand, however, the catalogue grew, and he had, from time to time, opportunities of studying the materials and the subjects they carried engraved on them, in other gem collections, more particularly in those at the British Museum (now enriched with the Blacas Cabinet), at Berlin, at St. Petersburg, at the Bibliothèque Impériale in Paris (including the Duc de Luynes' collection), and in the private collections of the Earl of Home (consisting of a part of the Montague collection), of Mr. Rhodes (including the Mertens-Schaffhausen, and Praun collections), of Mr. Heber Percy (the inheritor of the famous Beverley Gems), in England, and of the two Barons Roger in Paris. By the experience thus obtained, and by a still larger comparison of gem subjects, illustrated by a considerable collection of electrotyped and other casts that he has formed from several collections besides those named above, he was enabled to give the catalogue a more critical character than it had at first. It seemed but a natural if inadequate return for the truly gracious loan of the Collection on the part of the Duke, that a copy of this Catalogue should go to Blenheim with the gems.

His Grace, however, offered to have it printed in a shape uniform with Mr. Scharf's admirable catalogue of the other treasures at Blenheim Palace; and this proposal suggested to the author the propriety of putting the Catalogue into a more classified form, and arranging the descriptions in it according to their subjects. This re-casting of the Catalogue proved a very long labour, and even after it was performed, and the Catalogue printed, the descriptions of some of the gems, as seen in new light, after a second comparison with the gems, have had to be shifted to other than their original places; so

INTRODUCTION.

that numbers have dropped out in a few instances, while in one or two other cases they have been repeated.

The author is well aware of the incompleteness of his work. He can only hope that great errors have not found their way into it. Dates are sometimes, perhaps, too boldly assigned to the gems, and are necessarily, in most such cases, more or less conjectural; at least, they rest on that kind of induction which is, as it were, instinctively formed on the comparison of styles of treatment, or of the subjects treated on various gems or other forms of ancient or modern art; an induction which results in a sort of personal experience, which if it cannot always be supported by a direct appeal to the materials on which it is built, has generally more or less sound materials for its foundation. Of course the value of such an induction is to be measured by the archæological learning, the actual experience, the powers of observation, and the æsthetical faculty of the person who forms it, and the author is too well aware of the weakness of his own qualifications in these several respects. Finally, in saying that the study of the whole subject and the working-out of this Catalogue, have been entirely a labour of love and a recreation ; that in the middle of other and more engrossing duties, it has called into play faculties and tastes upon which the associations of scientific pursuits make little or no call, the author desires rather to explain the reason for the length of time that has elapsed between his seriously undertaking the Catalogue and his completion of it, than to shelter himself behind the cloak of an amateur against the criticisms his work may provoke from the archæological or æsthetical critic.

To many of his friends, and especially to the Rev. C. W. King, as well from his labours as an author of books replete with learning, as in the character of a friend always communicative of the lore he has gathered, the author of this Catalogue is greatly indebted. Among his colleagues at the British Museum he might name individually every officer of the Archæological Departments, the resources of which in coins have been so often opened to him by Mr. Vaux and Mr. Poole, and in gems by Mr. Newton, while the valuable stores of those gentlemen's knowledge and experience have been no less freely afforded him. To Mr. Newton he is especially indebted for many valuable observations during a careful inspection of the Collection. And in particular he has to express his obligations to Mr. Albert Way for the active interest which he exerted, in the first place, to obtain the consent of the Duke of Marlborough to the loan of his noble Collection. Of what he owes to the Duke himself for the confidence reposed in him in entrusting so valuable a possession to his hands, and in paying him the compliment of printing this Catalogue, the author can only say that he is conscious of the smallness of the return which he may be making for this kindness, if his Catalogue can add a fresh interest to some of the gems in the Collection it illustrates. It will at least remain as one among the many proofs that Blenheim affords of his Grace's care in illustrating the magnificent inheritance with which the public services of one, and the fine tastes of another of his ancestors have endowed his title.

N. S.-M.

CATALOGUE.

I.—MYTHOLOGY.

SECTION I.—THE GODS.

1.—*THE TWELVE GREAT OLYMPIAN DIVINITIES.*

Zeus——Jupiter.

1.—Intaglio. A head of Jove to the left on hæmatite. A Roman work of fine execution for this material. The stone has been re-polished in modern times.

2.—An intaglio on a red sard, representing Jupiter standing holding a long sceptre in his right hand; his eagle in the field. The work is rude.

An Arundel gem (Cat. Th. A, No. 40).

3.—An intaglio head of Jupiter Ammon, to the left, on a sard highly foiled. A bold Roman work resembling the head on some of the Consular coins.

A Bessborough gem (N. Cat. No. 19 C) originally in the Collection of Lord Chesterfield. Figured by Worlidge.

4.—Cameo cut in a nicolo, once covered with a film of brown, which is reserved to form a rim, and also survives on the paludamentum and eagle's wing. The beardless Jupiter, Jupiter axur,—a full-length figure, standing with the thunderbolt and sceptre, and the eagle, in the field. The Ægis envelopes his loins. The work is indubitably ancient, and probably represents an emperor, perhaps Augustus himself, as Jove. This figure is that designated as St. John the Evangelist in mediæval times. The famous intaglio at St. Petersburg, signed **NEICOY**, is similar in its subject.

A gem from the Arundel Collection (Cat. Th. D, 13).

[Jupiter Serapis, &c.] Nos. 5 to 11.

5.—An intaglio cut on the boss of a large pebble of amethyst, polished in its original shape. A front-faced head of Jupiter Serapis. It is Roman or Romano-Egyptian work of the finest type; the stone is 1½ inch in diameter.

One of the Bessborough gems (N. Cat. No. 14).

6.—Intaglio head of Jupiter Serapis, represented in full face, cut out of the black upper layer of a jasper onyx of which the base layer is white. It is rude work of the second century.

An Arundel gem (Cat. Th. A, No. 3).

7.—Intaglio head of Jupiter Serapis, full face, on a plasma of rich colour, a stone on which work of so much excellence is not common.

An Arundel gem (Cat. Th. A, No. 2).

8.—A minute intaglio, representing Jupiter Serapis enthroned; a sceptre is in his hand, the modius on his head, and Cerberus by his side. It is engraved in the yellow upper layer of a sardonyx, exhibiting also a white stratum, under which is a black base layer. The whole figure is not much above ¼ inch in length.

9.—Intaglio head of Serapis, to the left; a Roman work of the minutest dimensions, cut on an oval sardonyx bevelled away to exhibit a yellowish-brown top layer, which is separated from a grayish black base by a broad white band. It is a counterpart of the Isis (No. 45), but the colours of the stone are even more brilliant.

10.—An intaglio of the renaissance period, cut in a pale sapphirine chalcedony, and representing, in very rude workmanship, Serapis enthroned between Isis and Pallas within a zodiac, carried by Atlas.

11.—Confronted heads of Serapis and Isis; an intaglio of very late Roman work, on a yellowish sard.

> A Bessborough gem, from the Chesterfield Collection (N. Cat. No. 27 c).

12.—An onyx cameo, representing in profile the heads of Zeus and Hera, both to the right. A fine Greek work, cut in a translucent white layer, backed by an understratum of bluish grey.

> A Bessborough gem (N. Cat. 26).
> Figured in the "Marlborough Gems," Vol. i. No. 29.

13.—A cameo on a two-layered sardonyx; the subject a fine head of Jupiter ¾ face, looking to the right. It is cut in a white stratum over-lying a black base layer. The simple and massive treatment of the head is in favour of its being the work of an ancient artist.

> An Arundel gem (Cat. Th. B, 31).

14.—A modern cameo head of Jupiter, to the right, on a superb five-layered sardonyx. The uppermost layer, of a pale cinnamon hue, is reserved to form a rim. Under a white layer in which the head is cut is another brown stratum, below which a second white layer is seen resting on a base of black sard. The stone is bevelled to exhibit the beauty of its strata.

Associations and Attributes of Zeus.

15.—A renaissance, or perhaps modern copy, in intaglio on a sardonyx of the famed cameo at Naples, representing Zeus Gigantomachos, signed **AΘHNIΩN**. It is cut in a brownish red upper layer, below which are seen a white stratum and a base of dark gray. It is a fine work, and worthy of the stone, the layers of which are very equal in thickness.

[Europa.]

16.—A rude intaglio on yellowish chalcedony, representing Europa and Jove in the character of the Bull. Possibly a Roman work.

> A Bessborough gem (N. Cat. No. 109).

[Leda.]

17.—Intaglio on a dark sardine. Leda and the Jove-swan with Pickler's initial Π. The work and the stone are of a quality of which the subject is not worthy.

18.—A very small cameo of Leda with the Jove-swan by her side. Excellent Roman work on onyx.

<small>An Arundel gem (Cat. Thec. A, No. 136).</small>

19.—The same subject on a cameo of inferior workmanship : onyx.

<small>An Arundel gem (Cat. Th. A, 144).</small>

[Ganymede.]

20.—An intaglio on a dark sard. The eagle soaring with Ganymede. It is inscribed **KOINOY**. Probably the work of Natter, who used this signature. It is an intaglio worthy of his hand.

<small>Bought by the Duke who formed the Collection, from Cipriani; and figured in the "Marlborough Gems," Vol. ii. 42.</small>

21.—An intaglio head of Ganymede to the right, with the eagle introduced as a minute symbol in the field. It is a work of Burch, unsurpassed in finish, upon a superb sardonyx of three layers. The surface layer of a pale chestnut is cut away, except where it forms a reserved rim. The next layer of bluish white carries the intaglio, and under it is a base layer of deep brown sard. The beautiful strata of the stone are shown by its being bevelled, while from the depth of the reserved rim the impression stands out like a medallion. The gem carries the signature of the artist.

22.—A very fine cameo on an onyx, representing a head of Ganymede to the right, in a Phrygian cap. The relief is in a porcelain white layer, the base consisting of a horn-like stratum. It is a work very antique in its character.

23.—An apparently Roman cameo of the fine Imperial time, on sardonyx, in a bluish white layer. Ganymede feeding the eagle of Jove. A dark sard stratum forms the base of the stone.

<small>It was an Arundel gem (Cat. Th. B, 44), and is figured, "Marlborough Gems," Vol. ii. 43.</small>

Hera——Juno.

24.—A small full-length figure of Juno on a fine nicolo. She holds a sceptre, and in one hand a small conical object. It is good work of Imperial Roman age.

<small>A Bessborough gem, once Lord Chesterfield's. Natter (Cat. 34 c) calls it Liberalitas.</small>

Poseidon——Neptune.

25.—An intaglio, representing Neptune in full-length figure on a beryl, a stone so often devoted by the antique artist to maritime subjects. As in the Neptune of Cenchreæ and that on the coins of Demetrius Poliorcetes, his left hand holds a dolphin, in his right is the trident, and his left foot rests on the prow of a ship. In the exergue are the letters CL.SVP (probably the owner's name). It is good, probably Roman work, and finished with the " diamond point."

An Arundel gem (Cat. Thec. A, 42).

26.—An intaglio of Neptune, somewhat similar in position and in attributes to the preceding. It is engraved in a nicolo which has become much worn, and appears to be a work of rather late Roman date.

27.—An intaglio on a richly foiled convex almandine, represents Neptune in figure similar to the last, but without the dolphin. There is a hydria on the rock on which the right foot rests. It is a large and finely cut gem of apparently an early Imperial Roman date.

A Bessborough gem (numbered in Natter's Catalogue, 47).

28.—An intaglio on an inferior sard which has lost its polish, representing a bust of Neptune to the left. It is fine, probably rather late Greek work.

It was figured by Worlidge, in his Etchings of Gems, No. 31.

Associations, Attributes, &c., of Poseidon.

29.—Intaglio on a red cornelian, in which Neptune and Amphitrite are seen riding on a sea-horse. The work belongs to the renaissance period.

An Arundel gem (Cat. Th. A, No. 31).

30.—Head of a Triton to the left; fins are appended to the mouth, and the beard is represented as if wet. An intaglio of late Roman work, representing a rather uncommon subject on a jasper.

31.—Intaglio on an amethyst foiled to enhance its colour. A Nereid on two dolphins, holding or reining a hippocampus,—a beautiful but rather an extravagant work; stated by the third Duke to have been engraved by Natter.

32.—A deeply cut intaglio on a white chalcedony of a Triton and a Nereid (Amphitrite ?). The somewhat floriated tail, as well as the material, betrays a renaissance hand.

> An Arundel gem (Cat. Th. A, No. 32).

33.—A renaissance cameo, on a three-layered onyx : a Triton and a Nymph sport on the waves, with an elaborate background. These, with a Triton and a hippocampus, are rendered in a white layer of the stone below which lie a bluish and a horn-like stratum.

> A Bessborough gem (N. Cat. No. 27).

34.—A minute river-god reclining : an intaglio on a jasper onyx. It is somewhat deeply cut in the black surface layer ; a white and a black stratum are seen on the bevelled edge of the gem.

> An Arundel gem (Cat. Th. A, No. 91).

35.—A renaissance onyx cameo, representing a river-god in an opaque white layer on a black ground.

> A Bessborough gem, being one of those purchased from Medina of Leghorn (Cat. No. 22 M).

Demeter——Ceres.

36.—A cameo on sardonyx : it represents a head of Demeter to the right, in fine Greek or Greco-Roman work. The face is rendered in a white porcelain layer, the hair in one of coffee-brown colour, under these is a bottom layer of black jasper. In the hair is wreathed a chaplet of poppies, and over the head is a veil.

37—A veiled head and bust of Ceres, in very high relief, cut in cameo out of a beautiful amethyst. The date uncertain.

> A Bessborough gem (Cat. No. 10).

Associations, &c., of Demeter.

38.—An onyx cameo with a representation of Ceres seated and holding a cornucopia. Triptolemus before her, presenting what appear to be wheat ears, leans on the *rutrum*. A column with an urn fills up the design. Mr. King conceives the gem

THE GODS—DEMETER.

to bear a flattering allusion to Germanicus; Livia and Germanicus being frequently thus represented. The stone is 1¼ inch high; the figures are carved in a porcelain-white layer lying on a stratum of brown sard.

An Arundel gem (Cat. Th. D, 15).

39.—Abundantia, a head to the right, and bust with a cornucopia in her left hand, in intaglio of unusually good work for the material, which is haematite.

40.—An intaglio of very good Roman workmanship on a fine sard: its subject is Abundantia, full-length figure; wheat-ears in one hand, a dish of fruit in the other; an ant in the field.

41.—A singular "eyed" agate carrying an intaglio of poor Roman workmanship, representing Vertumnus or Bonus Eventus in a small full-length figure, nude, with wheat ears in one hand, and fruit in the other.

A Bessborough gem (Cat. No. 60).

42.—An intaglio on cornelian; Bonus Eventus carrying grapes and wheat-ears: the work is of the rude kind met with in the late Roman period.

An Arundel gem (Cat. Th. A, No. 95).

[Isis, &c.]

43.—Isis, or rather an Egyptian queen to the left, in the character of Isis, with the persea fruit on her head; cut in intaglio on a beautiful hyacinthine garnet. The art is rude but not archaic; it is probably Egypto-Roman, but may belong to the Ptolemaic period.

A Bessborough gem (N. Cat. 94). Natter calls the stone a Hyacintho Quarnacino, and adds " il se nomme aussi Berill; on appelle Berill toutes les pierres rouges ou jaunes, quand elles sont d'une couleur bien unie, et bien transparente; ceux qui sont d'un rouge foncé sont nommés Hyacinthi Quarnacini:" a remark which explains the peculiar use of the terms Beryl, Hyacinth, and Guarnacino garnet, during the last century. This was a gem of the Chesterfield Collection.

44.—An intaglio of Isis in a full-length figure of rude but perhaps Romano-Egyptian workmanship, cut on a convex garnet.

A purchase of the third Duke's; see Introduction, p. xvii.

45.—Isis suckling Horus; an intaglio of the same minute dimensions as the Serapis No. 9, the drawing of both being excellent. It is on a similar sardonyx; the surface layer in which the engraving is cut is yellowish brown, beneath is a white stratum on a base layer of dark bluish-gray jasper.

See Introduction, p. xvii.

46.—Isis; a female head, of very Hebrew physiognomy, to the left; an intaglio on the pale green jasper, often used in ancient Egyptian ornaments. On the head is the Vulture headdress, but devoid of the head of the bird: on the neck is an Egyptian necklace. The subject and the *carvesque* character of the engraving would point to an Egyptian origin for this elaborate gem. The treatment of the details, which are not of Ptolemaic character, would indicate a date for the work not earlier than the Romano-Egyptian period. Mr. King supposes it to be a portrait and even the signet of Cleopatra herself! But the Vulture attire invariably has, in the earlier times, the head and neck of the vulture rising from the brow —or this head attire is replaced by the asp's head—in the authentic portraits of Egyptian queens and goddesses of whom it is the attribute. Moreover, while the nose and face of this gem represent the conventional features of Isis, they are very unlike those of Cleopatra as rendered on coins. On the reverse is an Egyptian distyle temple, having in its centre the head and bust of Athor. A precisely similar gem on the same material is figured by Tassie as a cameo, and stated to have been the property of the Marquis Capponi at Rome. It probably is this gem; the place of which in the Blenheim Collection was among those acquired by the third Duke of Marlborough.

Apollo.

47.—Intaglio on a fine red sard. A head of Apollo to the left. Fine work, apparently by a rather late Greek artist.

A Bessborough gem. Natter in his Catalogue (No. 80) calls it a "Berill très bien travaillé."

48.—Intaglio, on a dull red sard, of the head of Apollo, to the left, a sprig of bay in the field. Fair Roman work.

A gem among the Chesterfield portion of the Bessborough Collection (No. 16 c in Natter's Catalogue).

49.—Intaglio on a dark red sard. The same subject as the last, to the left. The work is very rude, and of late Roman date.

Probably the Arundel gem termed "Pacis caput" (Cat. Th. A, 25).

THE GODS—APOLLO.

50.—Intaglio, on a red sard, of Apollo playing the lyre ; a once fine Greek gem of considerable size. It has been repolished, almost to the extinction of the delicate and shallow work of the intaglio.

> An Arundel gem : the Apollo Cithar œdus incidens of the Arundel Catalogue (Th. A. 43).

51.—The remains of a magnificent gem, like the last in attitude and subject—Apollo Musagetes—with the chlamys falling nearly to the feet. It is a Greek work of noble simplicity. The oval sard in which it is cut has been even worse treated than the former, the work on it having been nearly polished away.

> An Arundel gem (Th. A. 45).

53.—A very beautiful modern intaglio, on a fine sard. It represents Apollo much in the attitude of the "Belvedere."

54.—An early renaissance intaglio, representing Apollo with his bow and a spread chlamys, cut in a fine jasper agate stone, banded with brown and white.

> An Arundel gem (Cat. Thec. E, No. 27).

55.—Intaglio on a fine sard. A head to the left, probably of Apollo. It is a fine gem, that might have been wrought in Magna Græcia. The hair falls in beautifully worked curls, and the face is of the true Greek type.

56.—A deeply-cut intaglio. Apollo tuning his lyre ; on a nicolo of great beauty. It is probably modern, though Natter (Cat. No. 32) describes it as "ouvrage très ancien." It was a Bessborough gem.

57.—Intaglio on a fine transparent sard. The "placable" Apollo (as on coins of the Seleucidæ) holds downwards the arrow with his right hand, the bent bow being in his left. It is somewhat deeply cut work, perhaps Greek, but not very highly finished.

58.—Intaglio on a sard. Apollo Citharœdus ; in the field an altar. The work seems of renaissance time, the details not being in the antique manner.

> An Arundel gem (Cat. Th. A, No. 44).

59.—A small intaglio, on a fine oval sard, that has been somewhat polished down. A nude figure, apparently of Apollo, stands in the middle of the gem; on his head is a somewhat conical object, and in his hand he holds what may be a mask. His lyre, on the ground, rests against a tree on which sits a bird like a crow. On the other side is also a tree, with a similar bird upon it; and on its stem a female head appears as though part of the tree: perhaps Daphne, or Apollo's favourite, Cyparissus, pining away into a cypress out of grief for the slaughter of a favourite stag; or it may be only a comic mask. Beneath this tree is a hind suckling an infant (Telephus?). This curious little gem exhibits the characters of late Roman work.

60.—An intaglio, cut in a shallow manner, in a beautiful golden sard, of fine but late Greek work.

Apollo mourning the death of Coronis. The youthful god, loosely robed in the chlamys, leans against a tree, and mournfully contemplates the lifeless figure of the maiden, whom he slew on the accusation of a crow. The crow sits on a rock over her. Winckelman ("Monum. Inediti") calls this group Achilles mourning the death of Penthesilea. What appears to be a shield by the maiden's side is perhaps the result of a conchoidal fracture in the stone? There is at Berlin a paste with this subject, called ancient by Toelken, which had been in the collection of Stosch. It appears, however, to be really a modern paste, taken no doubt from this gem itself.

A Bessborough gem (Cat. No. 37), on "Berill," says Natter. Figured in the "Marlborough Gems," Vol. ii. 40.

61.—A cameo on a sardonyx, perhaps a Roman gem, reworked in later time, representing a laureated bust of Apollo to the right. The face is worked in a white stratum, the wreath and part of the robe being in a brown surface layer on a dark vase; backed with gold.

62.—A cameo, head of Apollo to the right, somewhat in the garb of a Muse; the hair, which is laureated, is done in a fine rich brown layer of a sardonyx, the face in a white layer, a translucent grayish-black material forming the base. The profile is beautiful, but effeminate, and Greek in character. The gem is $1\frac{3}{8}$ inch high by $1\frac{1}{16}$ inch.

63.—Head of Apollo, laureated, to the left, on an onyx. A cameo in a stiff style, and doubtless a modern copy, in which the hardness is affected, the fresh surface of the stone betraying its true character. The head is in a bluish-white layer on a black ground.

One of the Medina gems in the Bessborough Collection (Cat. No. 16 M).

64.—A paste cameo of Apollo's head, to the right.

THE GODS—APOLLO.

Associations, &c., of Apollo.

65.—A beautiful intaglio on a sard. A bust of Clio, to the right, with the historic roll of papyrus in her hand. It is figured in Worlidge. It may, perhaps, be a Greek work: the treatment of the hair, however, suggests doubts as to its antiquity, and it may be a modified copy from an antique original. There is a gem like it in the Florentine Collection.

> An Arundel gem, called in the Catalogue (Th. E. 23) " Semiramis— the roll representing her dagger." It has the same attribution in the " Marlborough Gems," where it is figured, Vol. i. 26.

66.—A Muse to the left. Intaglio on a sard. Rude Roman work.

67.—An Intaglio on a fine, long, oval cornelian; Terpsichore tuning her lyre. By her a cippus carrying a statue of Pallas. The antiquity of the gem is more than dubious; the style, though finely finished, being weak in character, and much after the manner of Marchant.

68.—A modern intaglio on a fine golden sard. Melpomene holding a mask; a cippus behind her.

69.—An intaglio on a very fine plasma. Melpomene holding a mask; a cippus behind her; in the field a shield and a falchion. The work, though not very good, is superior to what is usual on this stone in Roman times, and the form of the falchion confirms the suspicion thus raised as to its antiquity. It seems a cinque-cento work.

> An Arundel gem, designated in the Catalogue (Th. A, 60) as "Tomyris Scytharum regina," the mask standing for the head of Cyrus, and the falchion for the weapon of her vengeance.

70.—Intaglio on a fine sard, representing the head and bust of a Muse to the left. The letters **ΣΑΦ** have been scratched in at some later period. The lyre is introduced in the field with a bee. It seems to have been a Greek work of a late period of the art. Both Tassie and Worlidge have figured it. It is also represented by a plate in the "Marlborough Gems," Vol. ii. No. 5. It was in the Medina portion of the Bessborough Collection, and probably the mis-spelt lettering was added when in Medina's possession (Cat. 23 M).

Artemis——Diana.

71.—An intaglio head of Artemis to the right, with the end of her quiver showing over her shoulder; on a brown sard which has been re-polished on the surface; it is a large and curious gem of apparently early workmanship.

  An Arundel gem (Cat. Th. E, 7).

72.—A head of Artemis to the right. A cameo upon a fine sardonyx; the hair arranged with the κρώβυλος is rendered in a very dark brown sard upper layer, one curl however being yellow: the face, in a layer of ivory-white, is relieved by a fine sard background. The work seems to be antique.

73.—A full-length standing figure of Diana holding out an arrow, a cippus behind her; an intaglio in a beautiful hyacinthine sard. The work is exceedingly good, and if not Greek belongs to the best Roman period. It has been re-polished, but not to its injury.

74.—Diana leaning on a pillar, a stag in the field, on a fine transparent yellowish sard. It is a very rude probably late Roman intaglio.

  An Arundel gem (Cat. Th. A, 57).

75.—Intaglio on a sardonyx. The "Diana of the Hills." It is signed ΑΠΟΛΛΩΝΙΟΥ, a signature which is admitted by Köhler as genuine in the case of the small Diana on amethyst at Naples. This however is a modern work copied from the antique. It is cut in a layer of orange red sard, below which lie two strata of white and brown.

  A Bessborough gem; Natter's Diana Montana (Cat. 100).

Hephaistos——Vulcan.

77.—A modern intaglio on a beautiful agate. Vulcan at work shaping a helmet.

  A Bessborough gem (Cat. No. 103).

78.—A modern Italian intaglio on a cornelian, Vulcan's workshop, with a great many figures. The setting is one of a series in the collection exhibiting a delicately pencilled and richly coloured pattern of tulips and other flowers painted on a white ground.

  An Arundel gem (Cat. Thec. E, No. 1).

79.—Intaglio on cornelian, "Vulcan seated, a veiled lady by him; gives the sword and shield to a youthful warrior." Dr. Brunn considers it to be a copy from an Alban sarcophagus, with the marriage of Peleus and Thetis (Millin. Gal. Myth. t. 152. n. 551). It is a modern intaglio carrying a false signature ΑΔΜΩΝ. The white cornelian on which it is engraved was rarely used by the ancient, though it has been a favourite stone with modern engravers.

A Bessborough gem; described by Natter (Cat. No. 95), who omits to mention the signature, as Brutus imposing an oath on Collatinus to avenge Lucretia.

Pallas Athene——Minerva.

80.—A minute intaglio of a head of Pallas to the right, engraved with the point alone on a yellow sard. The gem is let into a small rim of ivory-white chalcedony. Like the gem No. 618, signed L.S., this gem is doubtless the work of Louis Siriers, a Frenchman who worked at Florence about 1740, and who received from Mariette the eulogy he was wont to bestow on a French artist. Giulianelli and St. Laurent also sing his praises. His works are frequently let into a little frame, in the manner here seen.

81.—Bust of Pallas, full face; a deeply cut intaglio in a large pale amethyst. It carries the signature

ΕΥΤΥΧΗC
ΔΙΟCΚΟΥΡΙΔΟΥ
ΑΙΓΙΑΙΟC ΕΓ.

In comparing this inscription with that quoted by Brunn from the MS., we find that in the latter it is continued in the form

ΑΙΓΙΑΙΟC · ΕΓΟΙ
ΕΙ

Its present form is explained by the gem having evidently been reduced by working down its edge all round, so as to form a bevil for the setting. The crest of the helmet is thereby apparently in part cut away. Possibly the original edge of the gem had been injured. An Λ and a second letter seem erased on the opposite side of the field. A doubt has been raised whether this gem is a copy of one of the best authenticated of the signed gems with which we are acquainted. The gem in question is described in a MS. in the Vatican, dated in the beginning of the fifteenth century as a head of Alexander the Great on crystal. The description is by Cyriacus of Ancona, who saw the amethyst in 1445 in the possession of Giovanni Delfino, a Venetian admiral. Stosch described and figured this gem (Pierres antiques Gravées, No. XXXIV.) in 1724; it being then in the collection of Prince Salviati Colonna, into which it had come from the cabinet of the Princes Salviati. Dr. Brunn supposes the Marlborough gem to have been a copy from the Colonna gem, which latter he states to have been transmitted, "as he believed," through the Collection of Prince Avella to that of Baron Schillersheim. It is not, however, now with the Schillersheim gems, either in the collection of the late Duke de Blacas, or in the collections of the Barons Roger. Raspe mentions a copy, but describes it as smaller in size, less deep in its relief, and inferior in point of merit.

The Marlborough gem was in 1761 described by Natter (Cat. No. 13) among the gems of the Earl of Bessborough. Natter, in remarking on its identity in all respects with the gem described by Stosch, says he knows of no other original, but suspends his judgment as to whether this was that identical gem. This language may suggest a suspicion that Natter may have had some reasons for affirming a doubt on the point.

Mr. King, in his notice of the gem in 1861, accepted Dr. Brunn's statement, and doubted the antiquity of the lettering of the signature. But he has changed this view, and believes now that this gem is the original. The size exactly accords with that of the gem in Stosch, as do the details in the minutest particular. Certainly, until the supposed Avella gem shall be proved to exist, and to have a better claim, this noble intaglio must be held to be the original of one of the most interesting of antique signed gems, and to bear the autograph of a son of perhaps the great Dioscorides. The engraving, though not of high finish, is of the boldest character. It is figured in the "Marlborough Gems," Vol. ii. No. 12.

82.—Bust of Pallas to the right in intaglio on yellowish chalcedony. Fair work of the Roman period.

 An Arundel gem (Th. E, 8).

83.—Pallas, a bust in intaglio, to the right, on a fine sard agate. Fair work of the late renaissance. The stone is a beautiful one of the oriental kind.

 An Arundel gem (Cat. Thec. V, No. 17).

THE GODS—PALLAS ATHENE.

84.—A cameo bust of Pallas to the left, on a three-layered onyx. The face is cut in a white layer, an upper horn-like stratum forming the helmet; with a base layer of the same kind. It appears to be good antique work.

A Medina gem (Bessborough Catalogue, No. 13 M).

85.—Minerva bust to the right, a cameo. Her hair is in a yellowish brown, her face in a white layer on a dull-coloured base. The helmet is otherwise only represented by the plume. Good Roman work.

An Arundel gem, termed, in the Catalogue of Lady E. Germain, "Caput Zenobiæ" (Cat. Theca, B, 11).

86.—A poor modern cameo on a sardonyx, representing a bust of Pallas, to the left. The helmet, shoulder, and hair in a red layer, the face in white on a red base.

87.—A bust of Pallas to the right, a beautiful cameo cut upon a stone as beautiful, a sardonyx, presenting a rich brown layer on a white ground; engraved probably towards the end of the cinque-cento period. The helmet is covered with a fantastic leaf ornament, carrying a mask on the visor.

An Arundel gem (Cat. Thec. C, 6).

88.—A cameo bust of Pallas to the left, of the renaissance period, and somewhat elaborate in its workmanship. It is undercut to give effect to the profile, which is worked in a thick white layer.

One of the gems bought by Lord Bessborough of Medina (Cat. 36 M).

89.—Cameo bust of Minerva to the left, on a sardonyx. The hair is rendered in a yellow layer, the face and neck in a stratum of white upon a base layer of dull orange; the cheek is just tinted with a film of the surface layer. The work is pretty good and probably of the period of Hadrian.

90.—Athene "Promachos." A late Roman intaglio cut in the upper layer of a minute nicolo. A crescent in the field is probably an astrological emblem.

91.—A cameo with Pichler's signature, on a fine little three-layered sardonyx, representing Athene "Promachos." Her shield carrying an owl is left in a yellow layer; the base layer is of dark gray.

THE GODS—PALLAS ATHENE.

92.—Minerva in a car drawn by two owls, on a yellow cornelian ; a pretty little Roman intaglio.

93.—An intaglio on a nicolo. A sacrifice to Minerva by a Roman warrior, perhaps Domitian. She holds out an owl towards him, the serpent being in the field as one of her attributes. Her shield is propped upon the ground.

94.—An onyx cameo. A helmeted bust of Pallas to the right, cut out of an ivory-white layer, on a bluish-gray ground. Probably renaissance work, or at best, an antique gem re-worked by a later hand. The stone is fissured.

Figured in the "Marlborough Gems," Vol. i. 27.

95.—A small head of Pallas to the left, helmeted, with a mask on the helmet ; in an ivory-white layer on a bluish-gray ground : the work is poor, and probably of the 16th century. The features have not the antique character, and are not those characteristic of Minerva.

An Arundel gem (Cat. Thec. A, 112).

Associations, Attributes, and Symbols of Pallas.*

96.—The head of Medusa (or of Perseus ?) in front face : a small and deep intaglio on a bright golden sard. It is beautiful, perhaps Greek work. A caduceus in the field.

Figured by Worlidge (No. 27) as a Mercury. It was a Bessborough gem (No. 18 c in Natter's Catalogue).

97.—A fragment of an exquisite cameo, representing the tranquil Medusa, more probably Perseus, to the right : a gem that must once have been 1½ inch in length, by 1¼ inch in diameter. In somewhat flat though not shallow relief, the hair and the wing are rendered in a rich brown layer ; a fine ivory-white layer of the sardonyx furnishing the material for a countenance of severe beauty. The gem is however much mutilated. The style is that of a fine Greek period.

---

* The myth of the Gorgon Medusa being represented in connection with the conquest of the mortal Gorgon by Perseus, and the assumption of her head by Athene as the ornament and terror of her shield, subjects representing Medusa, Perseus, &c., are not placed in a separate division, but are included with those which represent the attributes and associations of Athene.

THE GODS—PALLAS ATHENE.

98.—An intaglio on sapphire. Medusa's head in full front face; extremely fine work, and exhibiting a wonderful finish considering the hard material in which it is worked. The wings in the hair and the serpent's crest between the wings and round the chin indicate a comparatively late period for its execution. The sapphire is of a pale colour, and is mounted in an enamelled ring of the cinque-cento period, with arabesques and black vines covering the gold of the mounting. The engraving is probably a work of a good Roman time.

An Arundel gem (Cat. Thec. A, No. 1).

99.—Cameo head of the tranquil Medusa, to the left. It is cut in the white porcelain-like upper layer of an onyx, with a bluish-gray background. The relief is not so flat as in No. 97, and the presence of the serpent in the hair, together with the wing, betokens a comparatively late date for the gem. The beautiful modelling of the features, and the fine work in the hair, would preclude a date much later than that of Hadrian.

Figured in the "Marlborough Gems," Vol. ii. No. 10.
See Introduction, p. xvii.

100.—A cameo, of proportions almost sufficient to raise it into a work of sculpture. It is a Medusa's head, in enormous relief, cut from a large homogeneous boss of translucent chalcedony. The face is turned slightly to the right, and the expression in the eyes, brows, mouth, indeed on every feature, conveys all that art could embody of the "dreadful Gorgon." Every part of the face is as delicately modelled as if the material had been as soft as marble; and Mr. King has called this gem "the noblest work in relief that graces the collection." Six holes, drilled in somewhat divergent directions from behind, some of which penetrate in a concealed manner even into the recesses of the hair on the upper surface of the gem, held the fastenings that affixed this finest known *phalera* to a perhaps imperial corslet. A seventh hole is sunk into the back of the stone for some depth below the nose and upper lip, evidently to give a greater transparency and life to those features. This great work belongs probably to the age of Trajan or of Hadrian, if indeed it may not be assigned to the Macedonian period of Greek art.

From the Bessborough Collection. Natter (in his Catalogue, No. 1) remarks that the right side is cut en biais (with an inclination towards the other side) in order to give force to the left side.

101.—Medusa to the right, a cameo of beautiful but quite modern work, on a fine cornelian.

THE GODS—PALLAS ATHENE.

102.—A profile cameo of Medusa, to the right. The hair, in which the serpents and the wing are combined, is given in a black surface layer; the face in one of an ivory white, backed by a dark gray ground. It is fine work, of Hadrian's time.

103.—An onyx cameo, chiefly remarkable for its elaborate setting. It is a full-faced head of Medusa with wings. The date of this gem is very uncertain, but the form of the mouth and the work upon the hair have not the character of the antique, and probably it may be safely assigned to the last century.

104.—A front-faced Medusa slightly turned; a cameo, probably modern, and somewhat deeply cut in the ivory-white upper layer of an onyx with a dark base.

From the Bessborough Collection (Cat. 5).

105.—An onyx cameo of the Medusa's head, much like the last, and like it probably of modern work. It is cut in a porcelain-like upper layer with a gray background.

One of the Bessborough gems (Cat. 33 M), from the Medina Collection.

106.—A Gorgon's head full-face cameo, in flat relief, in an ivory-white surface layer with a yellowish brown base; the hair is rendered in this latter transparent under layer. The lustre on the hair, the expression of the mouth, the full unbroken roundness of the eye, do not bespeak the hand of an early artist, while the manipulation is superior to that of the latest period of Roman work.

An Arundel gem (Cat. Thec. A, 103), called caput Solis.

107.—Perseus with the Gorgon's head, viewing its image in his shield, while he leans against a column. A work of the renaissance period in shallow cameo on a fine sardonyx.

An Arundel gem (Cat. Thec. C, 19).

108.—An intaglio on a pale sard, signed **ΧΡΩΝΙΟΥ**. Perseus, an inverted sword in his right hand, head of Medusa in his left. A work of the last century.

A Bessborough gem (Cat. No. 99).

Ares——Mars.

109.—An intaglio bust, to the left, of Ares helmeted. A large intaglio, simple in its style and finely executed; its value is enhanced by its being still mounted in an antique setting consisting of a milled edge formed by the twisting together of two gold wires, which gives to the impression an appearance of an Etruscan border. It is engraved on a cornelian of large size, 1½ inch in height, and it is probably work of Greco-Roman period.

From Lord Arundel's Collection (Cat. Thec. E, 26).

110.—A beautiful little gem, representing Ares reposing; an intaglio on a yellow sard, either the work of a Greek hand, or a fine modern copy from an antique. A gem almost identical with it exists at Berlin, Class III. No. 380, of Tölken's Catalogue, probably a copy made in the atelier of Stosch. Another modern copy on garnet is in the Blacas Collection.

Described as Un Soldat by Natter (Cat. No. 44 c) among the Bessborough gems. Figured in the "Marlborough Gems," Vol. i. No. 38.

111.—"Mars Ultor," an intaglio on a fine sard, of very excellent Roman work. In the field is the inscription MARS ULTOR.

An Arundel gem (Cat. Thec. A, No. 46). It is figured in the "Marlborough Gems," Vol. i. No. 37.

112.—Mars resting on a shield; intaglio, on a sard, of fair Roman work.

An Arundel gem (Cat. Thec. A, No. 86).

113.—Mars, Venus approaching him, Hercules and Minerva on either side. An extremely rude late Roman intaglio, on a beautiful yellow sard.

An Arundel gem (Cat. Thec. A, No. 33).

Aphrodite——Venus.

114.—Head of Aphrodite to the left. Intaglio on a sard. A slightly worked but beautiful little gem of Greek workmanship.

115.—Intaglio bust of Aphrodite to the left, a large gem cut in a hyacinthine garnet. The hair has been carefully worked with the "diamond point," but the execution is not very fine and may be by a Roman hand of the early Imperial time, though the hem of the dress has a somewhat modern appearance.

20   THE GODS—APHRODITE.

116.—An intaglio bust as Aphrodite to the left, on a bright red sard, highly foiled. It is perhaps a portrait, the hair in particular is well worked, and it may be a gem of the early Imperial age.

    An Arundel gem (Cat. Thec. A, 7).

117.—Venus, something in design like the "Medici," on a very fine blood-red sard, unfinished. Probably a modern work.

118.—Intaglio head of Venus on a sard. A work of very dubious antiquity.

119.—A head of Venus in profile, to the left. A large cameo on a splendid sardonyx. The hair is partly rendered in a brown surface layer, the features in one of opaque white on a dark sard ground. The work is of the highest character and finish, and though somewhat undercut, may be of the age of Hadrian, or even of the early empire.

    One of the Medina gems (No. 29 M) of the Bessborough Catalogue.

120.—A pretty little cameo. A bust of Venus to the right. Carved in the white layer of an onyx, with a gray background: a finely finished and beautifully genuine Roman work.

121.—A head of Venus to the right. A cameo of dubious age; in very high relief with a wreath, probably of myrtle, in her hair, which is dressed in long ringlets and expressed in a surface layer of a rich brown colour; the features are rendered in a stratum like ivory; the base pearly white.

    Probably an Arundel gem (Ar. Cat. Thec. II, No. 30), called a Semiramis.

122.—Venus Victrix to the right : or it may be, as suggested by Mr. Newton, Artemis; with an erect javelin in front of her. A three-quarter length figure, cut in shallow intaglio on a splendid sard agate. The dimensions of this magnificent gem are nearly the same as those of two others to which in workmanship it bears much resemblance : both are profiles and both on similar stones to this. One of them is the fragment, the youthful Augustus in the character of Mercury, No. 387 in this collection. The other gem is a Pallas, a three-quarter length figure at Florence of a similarly amazonian type with this gem. The robe, as in this gem, is of a gauzy texture. Both this and the Florentine gem are probably portraits in

THE GODS—APHRODITE.

the characters of the deities they represent; the attributes of these goddesses being just sufficiently expressed, in the one case by the plume of the helm and by a ribbon-like adjunct of serpents to the slight drapery, while here the character of the Venus Victrix, or Artemis, is just indicated by the spear erect in the field before the figure. The features not a little resemble those of Marcia, but the work seems too good for the age of Commodus. The size of the gem, $2\frac{1}{4}$ in. $\times$ $1\frac{3}{4}$ in., and the thinness of the stone on which it is engraved, would militate against the antiquity Mr. King assigns to it, namely, that of the age of Hadrian, "the grand epoch of Roman art." On the other hand it exhibits a lustre due to a severe re-polishing, which so far helps to confirm its early date, if indeed this be not itself a part of a deception practised by a modern hand. It was, moreover, an Arundel gem (Thec. E, No. 4), a fact which removes it to an age behind that of the forgeries of the antique in the last century.

It is figured in the "Marlborough Gems," Vol. ii. No. 6, where it is called a Phryne. It was an Arundel gem (Cat. Thec. E, No. 4).

123.—Venus seated, holding out a wreath; on a fine Siriam garnet. A Roman intaglio of late Imperial time.

From the Bessborough Collection (Cat. No. 46).

124.—A late Roman intaglio on a pale plasma, representing "Venus Victrix," a subject of frequent occurrence on this stone. A vase with three ears of wheat stands in the field; while on her shield rests what may be her spear or a long flambeau surmounted by her pigeon; the drawing is of the rude style of a late Roman period.

From the Chesterfield part of the Bessborough Collection (Cat. No. 35 c).

125.—"Aphrodite Anadyomene," intaglio, cut in the red convex layer of an onyx with a white base.

126.—A sardonyx cameo of the Venus "accroupie," cut in an ivory-white layer on a yellowish sard base. It is a good work of the renaissance period.

127.—A much worn but once good Roman cameo, representing a Venus seated and robing herself.

An Arundel gem (Cat. Thec. A, 141).

THE GODS—APHRODITE.

128.—A sardonyx cameo, Venus washing her foot in a bath. It is cut in a white layer, with a reserved rim of the same material, with a yellowish brown base. It is a clever work of the seventeenth century, done to imitate the antique.

129.—Venus, or, perhaps, Hermaphroditus, copied from a statue in the Villa Borghese. A modern gem of poor work on a sardonyx, in which the mattress is represented in a yellowish brown stratum lying between a white ground layer and a surface layer, also of white, in which the figure is expressed.

130.—A cameo figure of Venus, of the renaissance period, in a contemporary setting. The design is of a voluptuous character. It is cut in a clear white layer of an onyx, to the transparent ground of which an emerald green hue is imparted by a highly tinted foil.

One of the Medina gems in the Bessborough Collection (Cat. No. 34 M).

131.—Venus at her toilet, with two Cupids in attendance; an intaglio of late Roman work, probably of the third century, and of no great merit. It is engraved in a black and white banded agate, which has lost its colour by fire, and is much fissured.

132.—From the back of No. 591. Venus and Cupid, a bow and quiver, and a branch in the field. Venus holding a flambeau; intaglio on a two-layered cornelian. It is highly polished, and doubtless of the same date as the cameo Diana of Poitiers on the obverse.

An Arundel gem (Cat. Thec. B, No. 22).

133.—A lovely little cinque-cento intaglio, on a garnet, of Venus drawn by a pair of doves; Cupid extending his torch over her from behind.

An Arundel gem (Cat. Thec. A, 59).

Associations, Attributes, &c., of Aphrodite.

134.—A remarkable gem, engraved in intaglio on quartz, backed with gold. A winged hermaphroditic figure, with an androgynous figure not winged, and Vulcan hammering on an anvil in the field. It is deeply cut, of a rude Asiatic style of art, and is supposed by Mr. King to represent the male form of Aphrodite, represented at Amathus as Aphroditus.

One of the Arundel gems (Cat. Thec. C, No. 23).

135.—An androgynous Venus, or a Hermaphroditus, erect and unveiling himself; an intaglio on a beautiful little nicolo, of good and minute Roman work of about the date of Hadrian.

See Introduction, p. xvii.

136.—A cameo on a two-layered sardonyx. Hermaphroditus seated unveiling himself, cut in a white layer on a yellow sard base. It is probably antique; the accessories being correctly rendered.

An Arundel gem (Cat. Theo. A, 133).

137.—A reclining Hermaphroditus. A Cupid in the field. A cameo of the cinque-cento time, cut out of a porcelain white layer resting on a black base.

[Eros, and the Erotic Cycle.]

138.—An intaglio on an oval convex quartz. Cupid propping up, with some effort, a huge cornucopia: an inscribed gem, with the name **AYΛOY** engraved in delicate letters on one side of it. The name appears to balance the design, and has all the air of antiquity. The design itself is spirited, though the workmanship is somewhat feeble; and the treatment of the hair of the Cupid is in favour of its genuineness. The gem and its signature might belong to the period of the Middle Roman Empire; the name indicating, it may be, that the work was after some masterpiece of an "Aulus." Against this opinion, however, stands the important judgment of Dr. Brunn, who condemns as modern both the engraving and the signature.

139.—Cupid; an intaglio engraved on an amethyst, very much in the style of Anton Pichler. The drawing and the execution are admirable, but show nothing of the antique manner. This Cupid presents in fact the features of the "Amour" of the age of Louis XIV.

140.—An intaglio, on a fine sard. Cupid running under the burden of a huge mask. An excellent work, of the best Roman period.

An Arundel gem (Cat. Theo. A, No. 53).

141.—A small intaglio, representing Cupid asleep on rocks, a butterfly in the field under his hand; perhaps typifying Death. It is apparently a good Roman work, on a pale sapphirine chalcedony.

THE GODS—EROTIC CYCLE.

142.—Cupid singeing a butterfly's wings. A small late Roman intaglio, on a hyacinthine garnet.

    One of the Chesterfield gems in the Bessborough Collection (Cat. No. 73).

143.—A cameo, in the boldest relief, cut in a pebble of bluish-gray translucent chalcedony. It is a head of Cupid; the hair characteristically plaited up the centre. The work is good, and probably represents the portrait of an infant in the character of Cupid during the time of the early Empire. It is an inch and a quarter in length.

    One of the Medina portion of the Bessborough Collection (Cat. No. 31 M).

144.—A modern cameo, on an almandine garnet. A head of Cupid.

    A Bessborough gem (Cat. No. 86).

145.—Head of Cupid, in extraordinarily high relief, probably by the hand of some cinque-cento artist. It is good work, on a variety of chalcedony, of a pale bluish white, endowed with a slight chatoyance, something like that of moonstone. The mounting is very pretty, consisting of "a pair of folded wings in enamelled gold, and an elegant open-work border," with a pearl under the chin, whereby the head of Cupid becomes improved into that of a cherub.

146.—An intaglio on a dull sard, of inferior Roman work; Cupid riding on a hippocampus.

    A Medina gem, No. 20 M of Natter's Bessborough Catalogue.

147.—Cupid driving a pair of horses in a biga, running on a palm branch. Very poor late Roman work, cut in the transparent yellowish layer of an onyx, with a white under layer.

    A Bessborough gem (Cat. No. 74), described by Natter, possibly correctly, as a Victory.

148.—Two Cupids in a ship; a small modern intaglio, on a lovely amethyst.

    From the Nuncio Molinari's Collection.

149.—A rude renaissance intaglio on cornelian. Two Cupids riding a bear, one rides and whips, while another teases the animal: a common subject with the cinque-cento and modern engravers.

    From the Nuncio Molinari's Collection.

THE GODS—EROTIC CYCLE.

150.—An extraordinarily beautiful little cameo, on a five-layered sardonyx. Cupid on a marine pard. The little deity is cut in a layer of yellowish flesh colour; the monster shows a brownish yellow tail and whitish body, relieved by a flesh-white ground. This exquisite little gem is undoubtedly antique, and probably belongs to the age of Hadrian, in which the polychrome qualities of these many-layered onyxes were much called into play.

151.—A cameo, representing Cupid in a boat drawn by dolphins. The treatment of the water is antique in its character, and the gem is probably by a Roman hand. It is cut on an onyx.

152.—A fragment of an ancient cameo, too fragmentary for the entire subject to be explained. A Cupid flying in the air, carries on a stick an object in the form of a parasol. A second Cupid, seated on the ground, apparently plays a lyre, and a third holds in his hand a (rhipis) fan in the form of an ivy-leaf. It is possible that it may have formed part of a design representing Hercules crowned by Cupids, or, as suggested by Natter, an androgynous Venus attended by Cupids: it is probably a work of the second century. The figures are cut in a white surface layer, on a base of transparent chalcedony.

A Bessborough gem (Cat. No. 50).

153.—A pretty little shallow sardonyx cameo. Cupid rendered in a white surface layer, with a swan in a brown layer, set off by a white stratum as background. The relief is extremely low, and probably belongs to the time of the Middle Empire.

154.—Cupid with his foot in a trap. A small, rude, and unfinished cameo of late Roman work, on an onyx.

A Bessborough gem (Cat. No. 71).

155.—A sardonyx cameo. Cupid sitting on the ground and playing the lyre. An admirable design, in a yellowish-white surface layer on a black ground. The drawing and the work, which is in rather low relief, are in the style of the second century.

An Arundel gem (Cat. Thec. A, 138).

156.—A curious little Roman cameo; whereon four Cupids, rendered in a white upper layer, are ranged on a grey translucent under layer of a convex onyx. One plays the Pan pipes, one a flute, a third the lyre, and the fourth, a merry little figure, claps his hands and sways his foot to the movement of the music.

An Arundel gem (Cat. Thec. A, 139).

26   THE GODS.—EROTIC CYCLE.

157.—A cameo, with two Cupids erecting a trophy; of admirable design, and probably of early Roman date.

An Arundel gem (Cat. Thec. A, 137).
Figured in the "Marlborough Gems," Vol. ii. 41.

158.—Two Cupids struggling for a palm branch. A vigorous little cameo, which is antique, but has had its surface re-worked.

159.—Three Cupids disporting themselves with two dolphins in the water: an exquisite cameo, cut in the white layer of an onyx. The figures, which are admirably finished, are in a white layer on a black base. The mounting is a broad border of enamelled gold. Microscopic figures of a Triton, a Nereid and Cupids, with Hippocamps exquisitely carved and enamelled, are in complete relief, while four table rubies divide the quadrants of this most beautiful jewel; a work no doubt of a great Italian master in the cinque-cento time.

This gem was an acquisition of the third Duke's; see Introduction, p. xvii.

160.—The renowned cameo representing the hymoneal procession of Eros and Psyche. The two child-like little divinities walk, side by side, veiled, even their faces being covered by the veil; while the boy-bridegroom presses a dove to his bosom. A winged Hymen conducts them by a knotted cord (intended for the Cingulum, or for the Nodus Herculis?); another winged Erotic figure prepares the nuptial couch, while over their heads the mystic basket is borne by Anteros, conspicuous with crisply curled wings. Dr. Brunn has shewn the incongruities in the design as estimated by the standard of antique custom. Such are the introduction of the dove, the veiling of the bridegroom, the covering of the bride's face, the treatment of the vannus, the use of the cord to unite and lead the pair, and finally the general distribution of the parts of the design, which is as it were confined between two parallel horizontal lines, instead of filling the area of the stone in the ancient manner. These criticisms must be recognised as fatal to the supposition that this exquisite work is antique. The lettering of the signature

ΤΡΥΦΩΝ
ΕΠΟΙΕΙ

is no less condemnatory as judged by palæographic criteria.

The history of the gem has been so far traced that a drawing of the subject by the hand of Pirro Ligorio, early in the 16th century, was among the papers of Bagarris, as recorded by Spon. The gem itself, which has all the characters of a design drawn in an age of proof prints and luxurious margins, must, moreover, have been Lord Arundel's property early in the 17th century. There can, in fact, be little doubt that we see in this beautiful work a masterpiece of the time that was familiar with the designs of Giulio Romano and of Marc Antonio. In point of *technique*, it has never been surpassed in any age. Indeed, alike for movement, for grace of form, for tenderness of treatment and precision of modelling, as for the delicate technical management of surface, this cameo may challenge any work of ancient or modern times. Furthermore, the tints of the sardonyx on which it is cut serve to typify the nocturnal purpose of the design : the figures being rendered in a dusky layer of a pale coffee-brown hue, seem to reflect the illuminating glare of the torch, while the ground is of blackest sard, dark as the night through which the half-lit figures seem moving.

Arundel Catalogue (Thec. D, No. 7).
Figured in the "Marlborough Gems," and by Tassie and by Stosch : and the design has been reproduced in all sorts and materials of art, perhaps oftener than any other similar subject.

161.—Psyche, a veiled figure, with a butterfly on her bosom ; her arm and fingers are just sketched in slight drawing. An intaglio on a yellowish cornelian, perhaps of the period of the Middle Empire. But this is a gem of which several repetitions are known. There is one at Berlin, another in the British Museum, and a third at Florence : and this is in all probability a modern work in imitation of the last. The head is to the right.

162.—Cupid and Psyche in procession. Intaglio on a sard ; very pretty work, but without doubt modern.

One of the Chesterfield gems (Bessborough Catalogue, No. 41 c).

163.—The Graces ; a group, with Cupid hovering in the air ; an intaglio on a convex garnet, rather deeply cut and extremely good work for the subject, which is generally rendered upon gems with inferior execution. The character of the engraving in this gem corresponds with that of the antique work usual on the garnet, and it and the design point to a Roman artist as its author.

A Chesterfield gem (Cat. No. 29 c).

164.—Adonis ; a modern intaglio of the last century on a beautiful pale sard with a forged signature **KOIMOY**. Fair work, perhaps by Natter, and clearly a copy of the much smaller gem figured by Stosch.

From Lord Bessborough's Collection (Cat. No. 98).

Hermes——Mercury.

165.—A noble Greek intaglio on a sard that has been wofully re-polished. Hermes walking plays the lyre. The figure, that of an ephebus clothed in the chlamys, the petasus hanging from his shoulder, combines the simple grace, the serenity, and the dignity of Greek design with the exquisite finish and modelling that characterise the Greek workmanship of the best period of Helladic art. It is all that remains of one of the finest intaglios in the world, and can hardly be of a later date than the 3rd century B.C.

<small>It is figured by Worlidge (No. 6 of his Etchings) as an Apollo! But see foot-note to p. xv of the Introduction.</small>

166.—A copy of No. 165 upon an amethyst. An exquisite production, in all probability one of two copies stated by Raspe to be by the hand of Burch, sen. He terms the stone a 'beryl,' probably by a mistake that might naturally arise from his description having been made from casts. The fidelity of the copy to the original renders it a marvel of the engraver's art. It requires much scrutiny to discriminate between the impressions taken from the two gems.

167.—An intaglio on a yellow sard, representing Mercury in front-faced figure. Clothed in chlamys and petasus, he holds in his hand the caduceus. The gem is figured and described by Stosch. It was once his property, but he sold it to Lord Holderness the father-in-law of the duke of Leeds, who, as a note in the MS. catalogue tells us, bequeathed it to the Duke of Marlborough. Its history has been traced back as far as 1589, when it was described by Montjosieu, in his "Gallus Romæ Hospes," and belonged to Tigrini. Spon described it as formerly in the hands of Fulvius Ursinus.

The figure is somewhat deeply cut, but like almost every intaglio of equal importance in the collection, has been re-polished nearly to its ruin. This gem is inscribed with the name **ΔΙΟΣΚΟΥΡΙΔΟΥ**. The lettering is large yet rather delicately cut.

168.—Intaglio on a pale yellow sard, Hermes Criophorus as god of herds. This is probably a copy of a gem once Stosch's, and now said to be in the Carlisle collection. It exhibits much exaggeration in the drawing: the signature **ΔΙΟΣΚΟΥΡΙΔΟΥ** as well as the work are doubtless modern.

<small>A Bessborough gem (Cat. No. 102).</small>

THE GODS—HERMES.

169.—Mercury conveying the infant Bacchus to the Nymphs of Nysa. It is very beautiful work on a jasper belonging to the Roman time. The figure is slight and graceful, and in a running attitude. The intaglio is not very deeply engraved.

See Introduction, p. xvii.

170.—Mercury, Criophorus, resting against a cippus; a rather small intaglio in a cornelian. Very good Roman work.

171.—A little figure of Mercury with his caduceus, cock and a tree in the field; it is at the back of another gem, No. 277, and like it, is probably a work of the renaissance period.

172.—A Mercury; a pretty little intaglio, on a rich hyacinthine sard. The god leans on a column holding the caduceus, and his emblematic purse. A cock on the ground by his side. The astrological sign Scorpio is in the field. Probably an astrological gem embodying a fortunate horoscope. Early Roman work.

173.—Mercury standing, with similar attributes to the last,—the crab on an altar representing Cancer, and like the last probably representing a favourable horoscope of "Mercury in Cancer." A fine intaglio, well worked, on a blood-red sard; belonging to the Roman period, but repolished in recent times.

An Arundel gem (Cat. Thec. A, No. 51), figured in the "Marlborough Gems," i. 36, and by Worlidge in his Etchings (No. 28).

174.—A striking little gem, representing the image of Mercury at the end of the perspective of a temple, which consequently projects on the stone. It is cut on a sardonyx of 3 layers, the image and inner end of the temple being rendered in a surface layer of brown; the five columns on either side of the temple are wrought in a white layer upon a translucent base of chalcedony, in which are four steps leading up to the temple. It may be questioned whether this gem be not a work of the last century. On the other hand the idea is antique, as is seen in the shrines of this sort that are found on Imperial coins; moreover the attitude of the little intaglio statue of Mercury holding the caduceus, and the surface of that part of the stone, do not look modern. Perhaps it may have been cut in Asia Minor during the reign of an early Roman emperor.

A Bessborough gem (Cat. No. 59): it is figured in the "Marlborough Gems," Vol. ii. 38.

175.—Intaglio heads of Mercury and Hercules confronted, on cornelian. Probably an athlete's ring; of late and very rude work.

<small>An Arundel gem (Cat. Thec. A, 82).</small>

176.—A beautiful early Roman intaglio on a very fine lapis-lazuli. Mercury presenting a purse to Herse, or perhaps to Fortuna, but the female figure is veiled, and without any of the attributes to fix this appellation.

<small>An Arundel gem (Cat. Thec. A, No. 52).</small>

The Olympian Assembly.

177.—A cameo of slightly oval form, of rather fine and very elaborate workmanship, on a singular sardonyx. The gods, as if in council, on a hemisphere representing Olympus. Jove in the centre, Neptune and Diana on one side, Venus with her Cupids and Mars on the other, behind her Mercury, and in the centre Apollo, who plays his lyre. The figures are in a white layer with a chalcedony background, while the globe is represented by a black portion of the stone. The antiquity of the work is certainly very doubtful. Mr. King considers it antique, in which case it would have to be assigned to the age of Hadrian or the earlier Antonines.

2.—MINOR DIVINITIES.

Dionysos——Bacchus.

178.—A good antique work in intaglio on a red sard. A Term of the bearded Bacchus.

<small>From the Bessborough Collection (Cat. No. 54).</small>

179.—An intaglio on cornelian; a head of the bearded Bacchus to the left.

<small>A Bessborough gem (Cat. No. 72) called a Plato.</small>

180.—Bacchus in front face. An early Imperial intaglio, cut through a white surface layer into a fine sard, which forms the mass of the stone, which is a nicolo.

<small>One of the gems from Lord Chesterfield's Collection (Cat. No. 43 M).</small>

THE GODS—DIONYSIAC CYCLE.

181.—Bacchus, a full-length figure of inferior and late Roman work on a sard.

A Chesterfield gem (Cat. No. 37 c) termed by Natter "une Bacchante."

182.—An intaglio on a burnt sard representing a Bacchus seated and holding out a cantharus. The face of his Pard is seen at his knee. A large and coarse guilloche border runs round the gem. Mr. King holds it to be a work in the archaic style; and it has much the archaic manner, but the rudeness of the border, and indeed of the gem itself, as well as its large size and convex form, give a dubious character to its pretensions to antiquity. If antique it is probably of Asiatic (Asia Minor) workmanship.

An Arundel gem (Cat. Thec. A, No. 85).

183.—An exquisite little intaglio on a beryl; a full-faced figure of Bacchus standing leaning on the thyrsus, and holding out a cantharus. It is in high relief, and beautiful as well in finish as in drawing: the work of doubtless a Greek artist. It has been wofully repolished, the right thigh and knee having nearly disappeared in the process.

An Arundel gem (Cat. Thec. A, No. 49); figured in the "Marlborough Gems," Vol. i. No. 33.

184.—A singular gem, being a figure represented in relief in gold appliqué on iron; it would seem to be a Bacchus, carrying a bunch of grapes on the shoulder. Metallic works of this kind are mentioned by Mariette as having been fashioned by an Italian about 1750, and palmed off as antique by him. Possibly they were made by pressing the gold into an intaglio, and then attaching it to the iron.

185.—A beautiful cameo on a sardonyx; probably a portrait in the character of Bacchus. It is a profile head to the left with long hair, crowned with ivy leaves. The ornament of the hair is reserved in a brown stratum, the features are in one of bluish white, the background being formed of a layer of sard. The interior of the stone has been perforated along its length: it was once doubtless strung with a set of Indian beads. The work is probably by an artist of the reign of Hadrian. It is $1\frac{7}{8}$ in. high by $1\frac{1}{8}$ in. in width.

An Arundel gem (Cat. Thec. C, 3), named a Berenice.

186.—An onyx cameo: Bacchus riding a panther and carrying the thyrsus; the figures are represented in a white layer on a violet-gray ground. The work, which is not very fine, is probably Roman of the 3rd century.

Associations, &c., of Bacchus.

187.—Intaglio deeply engraved in a fine sard, representing the front-faced figures of the youthful Bacchus with Ariadne, a Cupid's head below, and the fragmentary face of a second, and the head of a dolphin. All the figures are supported on the waves. The signature YΛΛΠY is seen in an open part of the gem that seems as though left for it. The gem is a large fragment, but comprehends the greatest portion of the design. Dr. Brunn contends that it is designedly a fragment, and throws doubt upon the signature on the ground that the □ is written in the square form. He calls it a Nereid and a Triton, but the vine leaves, and the style of the hair of the male figure, seem to designate it as Bacchanal. Mr. King, who has suggested Palæmon and Ino as the subject, gives his verdict in favour of the antiquity of the gem; the signature at least seems of the same date as the gem itself, but the letters are shallow, and coarsely cut with a broad wheel, and scarcely can be ancient.

The gem appears to have been one of those collected by the third Duke, and is figured in the "Marlborough Gems," Vol. i. No. 40.

188.—A fine intaglio of a head to the left of Ariadne, ivy-crowned; engraved on a sard. Beautiful Greek-like drawing, though rather sketchy in its treatment.

An Arundel gem (Cat. Thec. A, No. 9).

189.—The same subject, the head to the left, also on a sard; but the design and treatment is rather that of a good Roman artist.

An Arundel gem (Cat. Thec. A, No. 81).

190.—A remarkable sardonyx with a modern intaglio work, a sacrifice to a Bearded Bacchus. The stone is oval in form, and of the dimensions of $2\frac{3}{8}$ inches long by $1\frac{3}{4}$ inch broad. It is drilled from end to end, in imitation of the oriental agates and onyxes. The uppermost layer is of a rich brown red, the next is bluish white, of the kind that forms the surface of the nicolo, the lowest stratum is black. It is an interesting specimen of an artificially coloured stone, probably German; and exceedingly beautiful, as well for its colours as for the evenness of its strata.

From Lord Bessborough's Collection (Cat. No. 17).

191.—A very large intaglio on an agate of the renaissance period; it represents Ariadne deserted by Theseus, whose ships are pushing off from the shore: Bacchus is approaching, drawn by Satyrs.

An Arundel gem (Cat. Thec. E, No. 18).

THE GODS—DIONYSIAC CYCLE.

192.—A large and lovely intaglio on a sard, representing the bust to the right of Ariadne, or of a Bacchante, crowned with ivy: Greek or Greco-Roman work, but not of very refined finish. It is set in a row of turquoises, and the back is ornamented with enamel work of coloured flowers on a white ground, similar to that which adorns so many of the gems of the Arundel Collection.

193.—A cameo in antique paste of a Bacchus and Ariadne.

194.—A most beautiful cameo on a sardonyx, $1\frac{3}{8}$ inch × $1\frac{1}{4}$ inch; Ariadne, or a Bacchante, with a wreath of ivy in her hair. This and the hair are rendered in the rich chesnut-brown upper layer, the face and neck in a porcelain-like white layer resting on a bluish-gray ground. A delicately worked gem in rather high relief, and of grand design, and with all the appearance of its dating from the good Roman period. The head to the right.

An Arundel gem (Cat. Thec. C, No. 4), turned Dea Libera.

195.—A sardonyx cameo: Ariadne's or a Bacchante's head, to the left, perhaps Faustina the younger in one of these Bacchanal characters, with a spray of ivy in her hair. The ivy spray is wrought in a brown layer. The shoulders are clothed with the roe's skin, tied by the feet in front, and rendered in high relief in a surface layer of an amber colour. The features are given in a white stratum of this beautiful four-layered sardonyx. The work has the appearance of being Roman, of the earlier Antonine period. It is $1\frac{1}{2}$ inch in length by $\frac{7}{8}$ths.

A Medina gem (Bessborough Cat. No. 30 M).
Figured in the "Marlborough Gems," Vol. i. No. 31.

196.—A bust portrait, to the left, in the character of Ariadne. A noble cameo in very flat relief, on a beautiful sardonyx. The treatment of the eye and nostril is peculiar and rude. The features are thoughtful and evidently characteristic, and the hair is carefully but not very delicately wrought. These, with the neck, are rendered in a white layer of the stone, relieved by a brown sard background; the ivy garland, with a corymbus, forming its frontlet, and the robe with its clasp, are rendered in a surface stratum of yellow. A reserved rim surrounds the gem, which is bevelled off on the outer side so as to exhibit the beauty and evenness of the strata. It seems to be a Roman work dating perhaps from the 2nd century; it is $1\frac{1}{8}$ by $1\frac{1}{2}$ inch.

An Arundel gem (Cat. Thec. C, No. 1), Agrippina.

197.—A small cameo head to the right of Ariadne, or of a Bacchante, on sardonyx, in high relief; the face in a white layer, the hair in an upper layer of pale yellow, the base being also composed of yellow sard. It is good work, and may belong to the early Antonine period.

198.—A cameo on sardonyx, being a modern and well wrought bust portrait to the left as Ariadne, with grapes and vine leaves in her hair. The hair is partially, the vine garland and robe entirely worked in a rich brown layer. The grapes on the garland, and a button on the robe, are left in a white surface stratum, while the features, hair, and neck, are also represented in a lower white layer; the ground work of the whole being a stratum of rich brown hue.

199.—A head to the right in cameo of the same favourite subject, on a fine sardonyx. The ivy wreath and hair are rendered in a brown, the features and throat in an opaque white layer. The ground is of a reddish brown. The design is somewhat undercut, and in very high relief. Either a work of the renaissance, or of the early part of the last century.

A Bessborough gem (Cat. No. 9).

200.—A little cameo representing a sacrifice to the Bearded Bacchus by four Cupids. One of them holds a goat, one crowns a large goblet on the ground, a third beats a tambourine, and the fourth sings; a statue of the Bearded Bacchus in the centre. A minute and carefully finished renaissance work.

An Arundel gem (Thec. A, No. 145).

201.—A large shell cameo, representing a procession of Bacchus. It is a curious work of the best period of the renaissance, *i. e.* early in the sixteenth century. The design and grouping of the multitudinous figures is as skilful as the execution of them is minute, exact, and spirited. There are no less than thirty-three figures, including two oxen that draw the car of Bacchus, and a lion that marches at its wheel. Thirty revellers are thus depicted on a convex shell of 2 inches in length and 1¼ inch in height.

It was an Arundel gem (Cat. Thec. D, No. 12).

202.—Intaglio on a banded agate. A drunken Silenus, in an Etruscan border. He holds a thyrsus. It is ancient and perhaps Etruscan work.

203.—An intaglio of not very early Roman work, on a fine little sard. A drunken Silenus carrying a cantharus in his hand, and what may be a palm branch over his shoulder.

A Medina gem (No. 3 M, in the Bessborough Catalogue).

THE GODS—DIONYSIAC CYCLE.

204.—A stooping Silenus looking down, while a young Satyr pours a libation over his feet. Leaning on the right hand of the Silenus is a thyrsus, and the Satyr carries a cloth in his right hand. The design is enclosed in an Etruscan border, and cut with fine skill and finish on a black sard, deep red by transmitted light. The surface of the field presents an artificial roughness, but the work has the character of that by a good Roman artist.

205.—A Silenus procession. An intaglio on a cornelian; the details are very incomplete, and the antiquity of the gem is more than doubtful.

A Bessborough gem (Cat. No. 24).

206.—A fragment of an extraordinary cameo. A Silenus is pushed along by a running Satyr. The design is cut out of the ivory-white upper layer of a splendid onyx; the under layer consisting of black sard. A fine Roman work of the Imperial age.

An Arundel gem (Cat. Thec. B, No. 48).

207.—A small cinque-cento cameo, representing a full-faced mask of Silenus, cut on a four-layered jasper-onyx, the curved layers of which the engraving is made ingeniously to follow. It is cut entirely in a surface layer of pink jasper; strata of white, bluish-gray, and again of white underlying the pink layer.

Possibly an Arundel gem (Cat. Thec. B, No. 29).

208.—An onyx cameo, representing two Satyrs supporting a drunken Silenus, whose head has unfortunately been broken off. It is good Roman work, but much abraded.

209.—A cameo in low relief, cut in the white surface layer of an onyx. A Satyr lifting along Silenus in a state of helplessness; a Bacchante strikes the cymbals. It is a beautiful fragment of a larger Bacchic procession, and probably a Roman work of the early Imperial time.

[Satyrs.]

210.—Intaglio on a red sard, representing a laughing Satyr in full-faced bust, with a vine garland in the hair. A fine Greek gem, fraught with merriment.

From Lord Chesterfield's Collection (Bessborough Cat. No. 39 C).

211.—A rather shallow intaglio, on a fine plum-coloured amethyst. A profile to the left of a Satyr, extraordinary for vigour and character; his brows encircled with a vine wreath. A work perhaps of the early Roman empire; but more probably a copy from such a work by one of the great engravers of the last century.

212.—An exquisite little intaglio, deeply cut in a minute sard. Bust of a youthful Satyr in front face; it might be Bacchus, but that the ear seems intended to represent a pointed form. The face is looking up with a somewhat rapt expression, the head being crowned with a grape garland. It is wrought with the delicate touch of the late Italo-Greek artists.

> One of the Bessborough gems (Cat. No. 56).
> Figured in the "Marlborough Gems," Vol. ii. 13, and forming No. 8 of Worlidge's inimitable Etchings.

213.—Head of a young Satyr on red jasper; a rude intaglio of a late Roman period.

> A Chesterfield gem (Bessborough Cat. No. 28 C).

214.—A spirited intaglio, on a circular black jasper of cabochon form. It represents a Satyr, perhaps Comus or Marsyas, seated in contemplation on the nebris, his chin resting on his left hand, and his elbow supported on his knee; his legs are crossed, and between them rests his double flute. On the margin of the gem is the inscription **NICOMAC**. This and a precisely similar but rather larger gem in the Blacas Collection are probably modern works. This gem was an acquisition of the third Duke's from the Chevalier Odam, to whom it came from the Nuncio Molinari's cabinet. A gem with this signature is recorded by Duval as having been fabricated in the *ateliers* of Baron Stosch. The subject is not a rare one on ancient pastes.

> Figured in the "Marlborough Gems," Vol. i. No. 34.

214 *a* and *b*, are copies of the above, in a deep smalt paste probably by Tassie.

215.—This beautiful gem, almost ruined by the cruel polishing it has undergone at some barbarous modern hand, represents a Satyr garlanded with vine, raising himself on tiptoe, and squeezing a bunch of grapes with his right hand raised above his face. The juice seems to stream down into his mouth; he carries another bunch in his left hand. The splendid stone, in which this exquisite intaglio is cut in the delicate and shallow manner of the antique Greek artist, is a cinnamon-stone

THE GODS—DIONYSIAC CYCLE.

garnet, in the form usually given to this stone in antiquity, viz. "en cabochon." There can be little doubt that this glorious gem dates from the later period of Greek art.

An Arundel gem (Cat. Thec. A, 76).
Figured in the "Marlborough Gems," Vol. ii. No. 45, and in the ninth etching of Worlidge's volumes.

216.—A dancing Satyr, cut in rude intaglio on a brownish red jasper. The work and the material belong to the art of the late Roman period, and for that time the execution of the gem is good; for though rude and sketchy, it is full of spirit.

217.—A similar subject to No. 216, and equally rude, but otherwise much inferior to it in workmanship. A renaissance intaglio, on a yellowish backed sard, which has been much re-polished.

218.—A dancing Satyr; a modern intaglio on a cornelian, not finished or polished. It is, however, mounted in a ring with a beautiful enamelled setting of thyrsi and ivy leaves.

A Bessborough gem (Cat. No. 58).

219.—A Satyr reposing, leaning on a pillar, on which is a bust(?) and the roe-skin; in the field a Term supporting the Satyr's staff. The engraving is in rather shallow relief, and the design and workmanship are somewhat rude, but of the average quality on this stone, which is a beautiful plasma. The nature of the stone, and the style of the work, indicate a somewhat late Roman date for the gem.

From the Chesterfield Collection (Cat. No. 30 C).

220.—An onyx cameo, representing a Satyr with his infant on his knee. The figure rendered in a white layer on a black ground; it is undercut, and is certainly of the renaissance period.

An Arundel gem (Cat. Thec. B, No. 45).
Figured in the "Marlborough Gems," Vol. i. No. 44.

221.—A late Roman intaglio, on a sard, representing a Satyr sitting in repose, and contemplating a trophy of arms.

One of the Medina gems (Bessborough Cat. No. 1 M).

222.—A Satyr pouring out a libation before a Priapic Term. An intaglio deeply engraved in a long oval cornelian. The whole design is well balanced, and the figure of the Satyr pouring from his wine-skin into the (cantharus) vase at his right hand, as he sits at ease on a pard's skin, is very gracefully modelled. His pedum lies on the ground, and the thyrsus leans against the Term ; a crater is in the field beyond. The setting is one of the series of beautiful enamel work, tulips of exquisitely delicate workmanship, painted in enamel on a white ground.

An Arundel gem (Cat. Thec. E, No. 10).

223.—An old Satyr, sitting on a pard's skin, apparently plays the double flute ; an infant Satyr, holding a thyrsus, dances, while a Nymph, sitting by, waves her hand as though to mark the time. This pretty little family scene is engraved in rather deep intaglio, somewhat rude in its finish, on an extraordinary sard of fine red colour and transparency, and the design is surrounded by a granulated border. It is doubtless by the hand of a Greek artist, probably of Magna Græcia.

224.—A little festival, wherein a seated Silenus plays the lyre, a Satyr stands and blows the double pipe, a young Satyr bestrides a pard, while from out of an overshadowing tree, which with a vine on the other side forms a sort of border to the design, a second little Satyr looks down on the scene. Cut in intaglio, on a fine yellowish sard of a peculiar quality, transmitting a greenish tint. It appears to be a Roman gem of early Imperial age.

From the Medina Collection (Cat. No. 46 M).

225.—Two Satyrs playing the tibia ; a Cupid running to one of them. A rather large intaglio on a sard. One of the players sits on what appears to be a ram's skin. A work apparently of the renaissance period.

An Arundel gem (Cat. Thec. E, No. 21).

226.—A Bacchanal subject. A cameo, antique in character, wrought in a beautiful porcelain white upper stratum of a sardonyx, with a yellow base layer. The moulding of the limbs and form of the Mænad in the foreground, is extraordinarily delicate, and the attitudes of the remaining figures, viz. a Satyr teasing a panther, and a second Mænad, who is at hand to beat the tambourine, are artistically drawn. A reserved rim surrounds the design, which is set in an enamelled border of tulips and other flowers. The *technique* of this gem resembles the cinque-cento works, but the details betray none of the errors in archæology so characteristic of an uncritical age ; and the work is therefore probably by an ancient artist of a noble school.

THE GODS—DIONYSIAC CYCLE.

227.—A Bacchante on a fine red sard. A renaissance intaglio, a copy of the oft-repeated antique design attributed to Scopas.

An Arundel gem (Cat. Thee. E, No. 14).

228.—A very fine shallow intaglio, of exquisite workmanship, especially in the flowing drapery ; cut on an oval somewhat convex amethyst of a beautiful tint. It represents a Bacchante in extasy ; and in the workmanship no less than in the character of the surface it bespeaks an antique hand, probably that of a Greek artist of the third or fourth century B.C.

229.—A shallow and delicate intaglio, on a small almandine, cut "en cabochon." A Nymph (possibly, however, Diana), running, blows the flute ; a hound runs by her feet. Undoubtedly a Roman work.

230.—A beautifully wrought intaglio on a perfect little plasma of the purest translucent green. A Bacchante in frenzy clashing the cymbals, and abandoning herself to the dance they excite. The gem, which has been repolished, must have been a work of Roman art before its decline, and not only the drawing but the execution is remarkably fine, considering the date when the stone that embodies it came into fashion.

231.—A representation of Priapus worship.

232.—A Bacchante before a Priapic Term, a thyrsus in her hand. A good Roman, rather shallow, intaglio, on a fine, clear, yellowish sard. The work and the design are much above the ordinary treatment of the subject.

233.—A rude renaissance intaglio, on a beautiful tricoloured agate. It represents a Nymph sacrificing to Priapus, but is of very inferior design and workmanship.

234.—A Bacchanal orgie, with the signature ΑΛΛΙΩΝΟΣ, a Satyr and Nymph embracing, a Priapic Term in the field, and a Pan playing the double flute. It is an intaglio on a large oblong beryl, and is stated by Natter to have been the work of Flavio Sirletti.

A Bessborough gem (Cat. No. 22).

40 THE GODS—DIONYSIAC CYCLE.

235.—An antique cameo. A Satyr and Nymph represented in the white upper layer of a black and white jasper onyx.

<blockquote>A Medina gem (Cat. No. 25 M).</blockquote>

236.—A small renaissance cameo on an onyx. A Nymph assailed by a Satyr, but defended by a soldier with a drawn sword.

<blockquote>From the Bessborough Collection ; termed by Natter (Cat. No. 28) " L'enlèvement de Cassandre par Ajax."</blockquote>

[**Pan.**]

237.—A head of Pan, crowned with the vine, in full face ; a very fine intaglio for the material, which is a plasma. A work of the early decline of Roman art.

<blockquote>An Arundel gem (Cat. Thec. A, No. 5).</blockquote>

238.—Intaglio on a sard. Pan returning from the chase ; in one hand he holds a plate of fruit ; in the other, together with his crook, he has the skin of a roe or a goat that he has killed. It is a good Roman work.

<blockquote>An Arundel gem (Cat. Thec. A, 54).</blockquote>

239.—A fine undoubtedly Greek intaglio on a brown sard. Pan sitting, with a thyrsus leaning on his shoulder, contemplates a comic mask, which he holds in his hand. The work is deeply engraved.

240.—A spirited onyx cameo, representing Pan erect before a reclining figure of an aged man, both in a gesticulating attitude, as if in argument : intended probably to embody the idea of an author of the Satyric Drama declaiming, the Pan being introduced to express this. The figures are rendered in a white layer over a yellow sard ground. The gem is probably a work of the Augustan date. It is mounted very beautifully in an exquisite ring with masks of Satyrs on the shoulders, a work of some cinque-cento Italian goldsmith.

<blockquote>A Bessborough gem ; called by Natter a river-god (Cat. No. 101).</blockquote>

3.—*PRIMEVAL GODS.*

Chronos——Saturn.

241.—Saturn, his falx (?) in his left, his sceptre in his right hand. Extremely shallow intaglio, on a singularly streaked and smoke-tinted chalcedony. The work seems to be of the renaissance period.

An Arundel gem, called a Jupiter (Ar. Cat. Thec. A, No. 50).

242.—A head of Cybele to the left in intaglio, on a fine sard, or the subject may represent a city, perhaps the portrait of Berenice in the character of one. It is a gem of good workmanship; early Imperial, or perhaps late Greek.

A Bessborough gem (Cat. No. 69).

243.—A rude late Roman intaglio, engraved on a very fine nicolo, with its colours beautifully contrasted. It represents Cybele crowned with her towers, and drawn in her lion-chariot.

An Arundel gem (Cat. Thec. A, No. 73).

The Fates.

244.—Clotho with her distaff; a fine renaissance intaglio on a dark sard.

A Bessborough gem (Cat. No. 105).

Hades——Pluto;   Persephone——Proserpine.

245.—A good intaglio in sard representing perhaps Proserpine, if the ornament be wheat-ears over her brow, mounted in a heavy cinque-cento ring of gold, enamelled in black with the initials D. IHS. B upon it. The head is to the left, and may be a work of Hadrian's time.

An Arundel gem (Cat. Thec. I, No. 8) !

246.—A beautiful shallow intaglio, on a blue beryl, perhaps a fine Sicilian Greek gem, but more probably a copy by an excellent modern hand. Proserpine's head to the left is represented in profile without the wheat-ears, but dressed in the mitra. The artist's hand has worked in the shallow relief with much delicacy of touch considering the hardness of the stone. A gem identical in subject and similar in treatment existed in the Praun (Mertens-Schaffhausen) Collection (No. 1080), on an antique black paste.

247.—A fine intaglio on a pale sard worthy of it. Hades, enthroned, holds the sceptre in the right hand, a thunderbolt in the left. Persephone veiled stands before him. The gem is engraved with a bold and almost rough execution, but with much refinement of drawing, a combination rare except in Hellenic art. The drapery, done in shallow relief on the figure of Persephone, and deeply sunk on the lower limbs of the god, is very statuesque in its character. A certain confusion in the treatment, however, raises the suspicion that it may be a copy from an antique work.

248.—A small onyx cameo. A head to the left, perhaps a portrait, of the class, from the head-dress, usually called Persephone. A work of the last century; or, if ancient, it must have been reworked by a modern hand.

4.—DEITIES OF DESTINY; OF HEALTH; TUTELARY DEITIES, &c.

249.—A representation in intaglio, on a calcined sard, of a winged figure standing on the prostrate form of a man; of the rudest work. It is a figure of Nemesis; round it is the inscription, **TO ΔWPON NYNCHN.**

250.—Fortuna, holding a cornucopia in the left hand, wheat-ears and the characteristic rudder in her right hand. An intaglio, cut in a rude but effective style of art, in a rich brown surface-layer on a splendid sardonyx, the sides of which, bevelled away, exhibit the other strata of the stone, one being of a dark greyish brown, and below it a white layer. It appears to be a Roman work of rather late period.

Asklepios——Æsculapius, &c.

251.—A head of Æsculapius to the left, an intaglio on a fine yellowish red sard, with the characteristic Zeus-like cast of feature. The serpent entwining a staff is in the field. It is a noble gem, worthy of a Greek artist.

252.—Hygiea seated, feeds a serpent which entwines a cippus, on which is a tripod carrying a globe. An intaglio on a cornelian. Fine Roman work.

253.—Æsculapius and Hygiea in intaglio on a sard, a very inferior work of the renaissance period; or, perhaps, of ancient workmanship, but much repolished.

An Arundel gem (Cat. Thec. A, 55).

Cities personified, &c.

254.—Intaglio on a striped agate; a standing figure, with cornucopia in the right, and a serpent (coiled round his arm) in the left hand. It may represent the *Genius* of a city, the serpent referring to the city (?) he represents. The object in the left hand might be an Ibis, and the figure the Genius of an Egyptian city. The work is bold but rude, and in character like the late Roman gems of the second century.

An Arundel gem (Cat. Thec. A, 89).

255.—Head of Janus: a renaissance cameo on sardonyx, done in a yellowish-brown surface layer on a white ground. It is in the flat style of the earlier renaissance artists. (On the back is a medley of conjugated masks.)

A Bessborough gem (Cat. No. 34).

256.—A vast nicolo, 1¾ inch long and ¾ in. high, carrying a very rude intaglio. A central figure over which is a rude inscription, engraved directly, **OYPANIA HPA** seems to represent the Astarte of Libya or Carthage riding a lion, and with a sceptre in her hand. The Dioscuri (?), each with a star over their heads, stand, the one in advance and the other to the rear of the lion. **ΑΜΜΩΝΙΟΣ ΑΝΕΘΗΚΕ ΕΠ ΑΓΑΘΩ** is in the exergue,—"Dedicated by Ammonios for a blessing." It is of the rudest work, and perhaps an African gem cut during the 3rd or 4th century A.D.

A Bessborough gem (Cat. No. 4 M). Published by Venuti, and cited in the Corpus Inscript., No. 7034.

Hebe——Juventas.

257.—A shallow intaglio on a banded agate. A female, half-draped figure, drinking out of a patera; a type which, from its occurring on coins, with the legend **IUVENTAS,** is entitled a Hebe. It is an antique gem carrying an Etruscan border, and probably Greek work of an early date, perhaps 400 B.C.

<small>A Bessborough gem (Cat. No. 61).</small>

258.—A small cameo on a sardonyx. In the upper bluish porcelain-like layer is a figure representing the Roman personification of youth, perhaps a Hebe. The design not unlike the preceding being that so frequent as a half-draped figure in graceful attitude, drinking from a patera. The base stratum of the stone is of sard, and the work seems of Roman time.

<small>In catalogues of the last century this figure is designated sometimes as Semiramis, sometimes as Sophonisba, drinking the poison.</small>

259.—A winged "Hebe" by Marchant, and signed by him. A beautiful intaglio on a yellow sard, stated to have been copied from an Etruscan bas-relief in the British Museum. The figure is beautiful and highly finished, but in Marchant's long, slender, and somewhat weak style of drawing.

260.—An intaglio representing, probably, a Hebe. A winged figure, cut in a red sard, pours from an œnochoë into a patera; boldly handled by an artist of the later period of the Early Empire.

<small>A Bessborough gem (Cat. No. 75).</small>

Nike——Victoria.

261.—A head of Victory, laurel-crowned, to the left. A very fine Roman intaglio on a deep red (foiled) sard, but much spoilt by re-polishing.

<small>An Arundel gem (Cat. Thec. A, 80).</small>

262.—A cameo on a beautiful little sardonyx. A wingless Victory crowns a warrior in a biga; another Victory, winged, acts as charioteer to him. It was once the property of Cardinal Albani, and is signed by the incised name **ΑΛΦΗΟC.** The signature occurs in the blank left under the ground on which the chariot and horses stand, but its antiquity is doubtful and is justly rejected by Dr. Brunn. The whole group, and in particular the horses, is admirably drawn and executed. The gem is cut in a porcelain-white layer, which overlies the fine brown sard that forms the foundation of the stone. The work has all the character of a Roman gem of the time of the early "Cæsars," but the signature is probably a modern addition.

Figured in the "Marlborough Gems," Vol. ii. No. 47.

263.—Victory winged, or, perhaps, Helios emerging from the sea, in a biga; a spirited cameo: the figures in a blackish brown layer in relief on a white ground.

It was a Medina gem (Bessborough Catalogue, No. 19 M).

264.—Victory in a biga. A cameo on a sardonyx. The near horse and chariot-wheel are rendered in a black layer, the rest of the figures in a bluish-white layer, the base being formed of dark sard. The work is not very good, but the treatment of the horses and of the dress belongs to a good Roman period.

An Arundel gem (Cat. Thec. D. No. 14).

5.—DEITIES OF TIME; OF LIGHT, &c.

265.—A beautiful intaglio, representing a female figure moving forward in a dress fluttering behind her from her rapid movement; a tree and a Cupid in the field. Apparently it is not the entire gem. It is engraved in a Roman style of a not very late date, on a red sard, highly foiled. It represents the Season of the Spring.

An Arundel gem (Cat. Thec. A, No. 58).

The Sun God.

266.—"Solis figura," Sol; an intaglio on a "Venus-hair stone," (the Solis gemma of Pliny?); quartz crystal with rutile fibres in it. It is a full-length figure of the very rudest period of late Roman art. It is set in a ring elegantly enamelled with black, and with turquoise-blue beads.

An Arundel gem (Cat. Thec. A, 48).

267.—A similar subject, his whip in his hand, on a singular yellow jasper, its back being of a mottled green, whereon is engraved directly the word **CEMECEIΛAM**. This title ("Eternal sun") has generally another application in Gnostic amulets, being usually associated with Cneph or the Abraxas deity. The gem is of the rudest work and of late Roman time.

An Arundel gem (Cat. Thec. A, 47).

268.—An intaglio on a fine nicolo. Sol in a quadriga, a trident in the field. Roman work of a late time and of the rudest execution.

An Arundel gem (Cat. Thec. A, No. 41).

269.—Sol in a quadriga. Inferior Roman work, cut in intaglio on a sard.

An Arundel gem (Cat. Thec. A, 88).

270.—The head of the dog Sirius, radiated and open-mouthed, in front face. A very renowned intaglio, most profoundly cut, and marvellously finished in a material worthy of it, the kind of carbuncle known as the "Sirium" or "Syriam" garnet, as being obtained of the finest quality from the neighbourhood of the ancient capital of Pegu.

On the collar of the dog is the signature **ΓAIOC EΠOIEI**. Natter first described it in his "Traité de la Methode Antique de Graver," &c., No. XVI., and also in the Bessborough Catalogue, No. 40 C, and he acknowledges to have copied it. His copy, in topaz, is at St. Petersburg, and he has been suggested as possibly the artist who engraved this gem. Other gems with the subject, some of them certainly antique, but similarly treated, exist in different collections; one is in the Payne Knight collection in the British Museum, and another in that at Berlin.

The nature of the stone, one not as yet met with among the gems of the fine periods of ancient art; the execution and finish of the work, too perfect for comparison with ancient works on the almandine garnets of Greece and Rome; the presence of the collar carrying a signature which too little inspires confidence in its antiquity—all have been urged as marking this Bessborough star-dog with a modern stamp. It has, however, the valuable opinion of Dr. Brunn in its favour, notwithstanding Köhler's criticisms, and under any circumstances it must for ever remain in that small class of magnificent works of which the nuptials of Cupid and Psyche, in this collection, is another example, that possess an intrinsic value, to be measured rather by their extraordinary merit than by the antiquarian interest involved in their date. The observations upon No. 713 may tend to strengthen the belief that Natter was the master who engraved it; but his language in his book is quite incompatible with such a belief. It was, moreover, one of Lord Chesterfield's gems, and there is no reason to suppose that Natter engraved any of the works in that Collection.

Eos——Aurora.

271.—Aurora in a biga, clad with the arching veil of the antique ΗΩΣ. It is wrought on a sardonyx in extraordinary relief, and with transcendent excellence. Though unhappily so much injured as to be but a fragment, it represents a large portion of perhaps the finest of the many cameos with its subject in the world. The near horse must once have been carved nearly "in the round," for it almost prances in the air. Unfortunately the undercutting, essential to the bold relief of the head and two of the legs of this delicately modelled horse, has exposed them to the accident from which they and the spokes of the chariot-wheel have suffered; perhaps arising from some unskilled hand having sought to take a cast of the figures in an unfit material. The axle of the chariot carries a minute silver stud. The material might have been chosen to represent the subject, the figures being carved in a most beautiful ivory-like layer, while the background, over which they are moving, is a yellow sard, that might express the amber light of the opening morning. What is its date? if it be not Siculo-Greek, the alternative can only be the cinque-cento time. The former is the more probable.

<small>It was one of the Arundel gems (Cat. Thec. B, No. 41).
Figured in the "Marlborough Gems," Vol. ii. No. 39.</small>

272.—In this fine cameo we have the same subject very similarly treated, but the relief is flat in comparison with the last. In each the figure and garb of Aurora are quite similar, and she holds the reins in her two hands in the same way. Indeed the two gems might both have been copies from the same original. This beautiful gem is cut in a jasper onyx, hardly less appropriate in the accordance of the colours of the stone with the subject represented than the last; the figures, carved in a wax-like layer, present a more dusky hue, and seem emerging from the night; the background of the gem being formed of a layer of blackest jasper. One can hardly assign to this gem a later date than that of the Rome of Augustus.

<small>An Arundel gem (Cat. Thec. C, No. 21).
Figured in the "Marlborough Gems," Vol. ii. No. 48.</small>

273.—Phaethon, his chariot and horses, represented in the white layer of an onyx; in slight relief, the transparent ground layer of the stone being highly foiled, with a crimson back. It is a pretty renaissance work.

One of the Medina gems (Cat. No. 39 M).

6.—ASTROLOGICAL SUBJECTS OF PAGAN CHARACTER.

274.—A triumphal car, surrounded by all the signs of the zodiac. A Victory holding out a wreath, floats in the air over a quadriga. The gem is finished in minute detail, though in rather rude work, and is contained in a minute sard of circular form and of a somewhat obscure yellow-brown colour, the diameter of which is but ⅝ths of an inch. Baron Roger de Sivry possesses in his collection a gem in all respects similar to this.

Figured in Worlidge's Etchings, No. 39.

275.—A renaissance copy of a subject of which a representation exists on a gem in the French imperial cabinet. Jove with his eagle, and with Mercury on the one hand, and Mars on the other, stands on a hemispherical frame, below which Neptune with his trident raises half his form from out of the ocean. Around the whole is a zodiac. The intaglio is cut in a large cornelian of 1¾ inch in diameter, and no doubt represents a horoscope.

The mounting is an elaborate production of an Italian artist, the stone being set round with table diamonds and spinel rubies, interspersed with enamelled roses, and other flowers, and suspended by a chain. On the back is a representation, in richly coloured enamel, of a stork-shaped imaginary bird.

An Arundel gem (Cat. Thec. E, No. 11).

276.—An intaglio on an agate. A singular design to which it is difficult to attach any meaning, as the Greek letters inscribed over the figures convey no sense, and the figures themselves represent no very assignable deities. A winged female goddess and a Cupid are in the centre; on one side a figure apparently meant for Apollo, and another playing Pan's pipes; two unrecognisable personages are on the other side.

From the Bessborough Collection. It is stated by Natter (Cat. No. 23) to have been previously in the Collection of Mr. Stanhope.

277.—An astrological medley. Venus with Cupid ; in the field the symbols of Libra, Venus, Jupiter, and Mercury (?). In her hand Venus also holds a pair of scales. It is an intaglio of renaissance work on a most curious sard, with a green hue by reflected and a red by transmitted light, having a white vein running athwart it. The Mercury (No. 171) is at the back of it.

7.—MITHRAIC SUBJECTS.

278.—An intaglio on a hæmatite. An amulet, very curious on account of the combination, probably not accidental, of the Mithraic subject on the obverse with an Abraxas on the reverse. The former is the usual representation of Mithras slaughtering the bull ; the crab and a serpent below in the field, besides an eagle, a jackal, two altars, and two heads. The style is very rude, and though far superior to that of the majority of these talismans, it is still too imperfect to allow of a very accurate description ; it is no doubt a work of the second century. For the intaglio on the reverse see No. 287.

279.—A renaissance rendering of the last design, but it is without the proper attributes of the Mithraic subject of it, and would be more correctly, perhaps, described as a wingless Victory sacrificing a bull. It is an intaglio well cut on a cornelian, and is set in a very pretty renaissance seal.

A Bessborough gem (Cat. No. 106).

280.—A Mithraic subject in intaglio, on bloodstone. Perhaps the Soul and the two Principles, and is much like the gem in the Praun Collection, figured in p. 359 of Mr. King's work on antique gems. A work of perhaps the first century.

One of the Chesterfield gems in the Bessborough Collection (Cat. No. 38 c).

8.—EGYPTIAN SUBJECTS.*

281.—A Horus Harpocrates seated in the boat of the Sun on a lotus flower, wearing the disc of the sun, raising his left hand to his mouth, and holding in his right a whip ; adored by a Cynocephalus, wearing on his head a disc (sacred to the moon). At the prow and stern a hawk, the emblem of Horus, crowned

---

* For Isis, see under Demeter, Nos. 43 to 46 ; and for Serapis, see under Zeus, Nos. 5 to 11.

with Pschent (the crown of the upper and lower world); in the field the sun and moon. It is a well cut Romano-Egyptian intaglio, on a curious jasper of a dull brownish red, with a stain of green in it.

  An Arundel gem (Cat. Thec. A, No. 99).

282.—Harpocrates. A full-length figure in intaglio, on a splendid red sard. His finger on his lip (as a divinity of Silence), he holds in his left hand a cornucopia, resting on a column. On his head is the persea fruit. It is a fine work of Romano-Egyptian art.

283.—A seated Harpocrates, his forefinger on his lip, his left hand holding the cornucopia: the right foot is broken. A cameo in the highest relief, cut in a fine porcelain white layer of a fine sardonyx, the lower layer consisting of red brown sard. The modelling of the figure is delicate, and the finish of the work excellent. It is somewhat undercut, and otherwise of a modern aspect, and must be considered a cinque-cento copy from a Romano-Egyptian antique, or more probably as such an antique gem re-worked in the sixteenth century.

  An Arundel gem (Cat. Thec. B, No. 43).

284.—A very fine copy, probably by Natter, of the Sphinx of Thamyras, in the Blacas Collection. It is an intaglio on a most magnificent sard.

  A Bessborough gem (Cat. No. 92).

285.—A Canopic vase; a head rising from it, covered with the head-dress of Osiris. Probably, on this account, of Roman time, as the Egyptian representation of this subject has the heads of four divinities in place of the Osiris head. Such vases appear to have been used to contain the intestines of the deceased. The intaglio is cut in the brown upper layer of a convex sardonyx, with an underlayer of white. An inscription, ΦΙΛΙΠ ΠΟΥ doubtless the owner's name, surrounds the vase, on which arabesque-looking ornaments are seen. The work is ancient, though the gem has been much re-polished. It is probably a work of late Romano-Egyptian art.

  An Arundel gem (Cat. Thec. A, No. 83).

286.—The same subject, finely engraved on a cinnamon stone of great beauty. The vase has hieroglyphics on it. Its date is probably coeval with the last.

9.—GNOSTIC SUBJECTS.

287.—The figure of Abrasax (Abraxas); **ΙΑΩ** on a shield on his right, a scourge in his left hand. The figure, cut in hæmatite, is evidently meant not for a seal but for a talisman, and it and the letters are therefore not inverted in the intaglio. This is the gem engraved at the back of the Mithraic Bull, No. 278.

288.—The figure of the same mystic form. The cock's head is more plain than in the last, and like that it has the serpent formed lower extremities. It is cut in shallow intaglio, on the back of the fine nicolo, which has the head of Commodus on its obverse, No. 480; and it was doubtless placed there to convert that great gem into an amulet. Around the figure are in Greek letters the words written directly **ΑΡΔΟΥ ΓΕΝΝΑΙ ΩΔΕΜΕΝΙ ΒΑΣΙΛΙΣΚΩΣ**. The work is good for a subject of this class.

289.—Intaglio on a mottled plasma; a radiated lion-headed serpent rising in the air from his coiled tail; the figure representing Cneph,—**ΧΝΟΥΦΙΣ**. At the back is a symbol, the three *f*'s, or ₩, conferring the talismanic influences of an amulet on a gem otherwise Egyptian. Around the figure of Cnoubis (the Creator in the Egyptian system, and a Demiurgus in that of the Gnostics) are the words in direct Greek characters, **ΧΝΟΥΜΙC ΓΙΓΑΝΤΟΠΛΗΚΤΑ ΒΑΡΩΦΙΤΑ**, "Cnoumis, the giant-defeater." The date of the gem is probably the third century.

A Bessborough gem (Cat. No. 33).

290.—An amulet with three K's, with a Coptic inscription in direct Greek characters, **ΘΩΒΑΡΡΑΒΑΥΔΡΥΩΣΣ**. A Gnostic work of the fourth century; at the back of the Hercules strangling a lion, No. 302, intaglio in red jasper. This amulet is that prescribed by Alexander of Tralles, as a charm against the colic.

An Arundel gem (Cat. Thec. A. No. 87).

Section II.—THE HEROES.

1.—*HERACLEAN CYCLE.*

291.—A fragment of a head of Hercules to the left, very skilfully made up in gold. It is a very deep intaglio, of the "Glycon" type, and perhaps of Greek work, in a most simple and grand style, in a cornelian, and was once a gem of large size.

An Arundel gem (Cat. Thec. E, No. 29).

292.—A head of Hercules to the left, of very late Roman work, on a burnt sard.

Figured No. 20 of Worlidge's Etchings.

293.—Intaglio on a good sard. The same subject to the left, treated in a rude but more formal manner by apparently a very late artist of the Empire: a wreath, probably meant for poplar, on the head. It may be a portrait of a late emperor, perhaps of Maximian, as Hercules.

An Arundel gem (Cat. Thec. A, No. 38).

294.—Head of the youthful Hercules, to the left; an intaglio on a fine sard. It has a very modern appearance, perhaps from having been re-worked, but the face and the hair have an antique character.

A Bessborough gem, Chesterfield portion (Cat. No. 13 c).

295.—Hercules mingens; very inferior and late Roman work, in intaglio, on a greyish coloured agate.

See Introduction, p. xvii.

296.—The celebrated Hercules bibax, with the lettering **AΔMΩN** behind the figure, which is a full-length side figure to the left carrying a vast club. The signature, which seems ancient, and fills a place evidently left for it in the design, would be limited by the form of the ω to the Roman Period. Indeed, the heaviness of the figure belongs to a time much later than even the original of the Farnese Hercules; the early athletic type of Hercules degenerating into more massive and clumsy exaggerations as we trace it down from the older Greek to the later Roman artists. It may even be a work of Caracalla's time.

THE HEROES—HERACLEAN CYCLE.

This fine gem is cut in not very deep intaglio on a slightly convex sard; the lettering, besides being in the nominative, is too large to be the signature of the artist, and no doubt, as Dr. Brunn supposes, represents the name of the owner. A gem with this design (figured by Stosch) belonged to the Collection of Vitelleschi Verospi; another figured by Worlidge (in 1768), (No. 21) was this, of the Marlborough Collection. Bracci and Visconti speak of such a gem as in the Nuncio Molinari's Collection, a statement considered by Dr. Brunn to militate against the Marlborough gem being that of the Verospi Cabinet. Raspe, however, states that this gem came to the Duke of Marlborough's Collection from that of Molinari, into which it had passed, he says, from the Verospi Cabinet.

A careful comparison of this gem and that in the Blacas Collection shows this to be the finer and more antique looking work. The Blacas gem, however, is on a finer stone, by no means always an evidence of antiquity; and it accords better with the drawing in Stosch. It is doubtful which is the original, though if Raspe's statement may be relied on, it must be the Marlborough gem.

Figured in the "Marlborough Gems," Vol. i. No. 32.

297.—A full-length front figure of the youthful Hercules, with the hide of the lion on one arm, the club in the hand of the other. A most excellent intaglio, of the best period of Roman work, on a superb red sard, perfect as well in its transparency as in its colour.

298.—Hercules reposing; the subject of the Colossus at Tarentum, brought to Rome by Fabius, and originally executed by Lysippus. Other copies exist with the motto ΠΟΝΟΣ ΤΟΥ ΚΑΛΩΣ ΗΣΥΧΑΖΕΙΝ ΑΙΤΙΟΣ. One was in the Orleans Collection. That this intaglio is not ancient may be concluded from the curve of the bow, and the treatment of the other accessories, no less than from the material, which is bloodstone; a mineral never employed by the Roman art of that early time, to which alone this class of work, if ancient, must have been referred.

An Arundel gem (Cat. Thec. E, 13).

299.—The same subject, on what looks like an antique stone, a red sard. The intaglio is an unfinished work, being unpolished, but it is of good execution, and probably an old design taken in hand and improved by a modern artist.

300.—A modern intaglio of the same subject, stated to have been the work of Natter. It is, however, not very good work, on a white cornelian.

See Introduction, p. xvii.

54 THE HEROES—HERACLEAN CYCLE.

301.—A mediocre Roman intaglio, representing Hercules wrestling with Antæus, on a fine little lapis lazuli, somewhat convex, and in good condition for that stone. It is mounted in a beautiful ring, with a white enamelled fleur-de-lis, and black arabesque work of entwined vines.

An Arundel gem (Cat. Thec. A, 56).

302.—Hercules strangling the lion, a rude intaglio on a brick-red jasper; on the back is an amulet, see No. 290. It is very late Roman work, perhaps contemporary with the Gnostic amulet on the reverse, and therefore possibly as late as the fourth century.

An Arundel gem (Cat. Thec. A, No. 87). This gem was once in the Collection of Gorlæus (see No. 441 Gorlæi Dactylotheca), afterwards purchased by King James I. for his son.

303.—Hercules supporting Antiope, the dying Queen of the Amazons. A modern intaglio copy on sard of this frequent subject.

304.—Intaglio on a magnificent dark sard. Hercules having brought back Alcestis from the shades, presents her to her astonished husband. This is perhaps the chef d'œuvre of Marchant, and exhibits at once the excellencies and the imperfections of his style. The graceful form of the wife stands in contrast with the erect demi-god, who, raising the veil of Alcestis, gives her back to Admetus. The figure of Admetus is more feeble in design, and the proportion of the head is in each figure too small. But though with little of the austere spirit of antique art, the conception of the gem is good, recalling somewhat the motive of the gem numbered 9211 in Tassie; the heralds leading off Briseis. Work so finished was impossible, except in an age supplied with lenses of high power. This fine gem was a present from the Elector Duke of Saxony, in return for a copy of the "Marlborough Gems," presented to his Serene Highness by the third Duke of Marlborough. On the back of the gem an inscription, in beautifully cut letters, "Saxoniæ Princeps doni memor," commemorates the occasion of so princely a gift.

305.—Head of Hercules in full face. A cameo in hyacinthine garnet, with much the appearance of being a late Roman work, but it is very difficult to judge of the date of such camei.

306.—A cameo cut in a white layer with a dark ground. Hercules bibax, with Lilliputian Cupids (in imitation of the old subject of Hercules and the Pygmies?); of rude design, and cinque cento workmanship.

An Arundel gem (Cat. Thec. D, No. 16).

THE HEROES—HERACLEAN CYCLE.

307.—Hercules; a minute modern cameo, the letters **HPAK** in the field: in a bluish-white layer on a black base. Stated by the Duke of Marlborough to have been the work of Burch (in a note to the Blenheim Catalogue).

308.—Hercules strangling the lion; a large cameo on an onyx. A very spirited antique work.

Figured in the "Marlborough Gems," Vol. ii. No. 44.

309.—A full-faced cameo, bust of Hercules. It has been worked (in the cinque-cento period) in order to take advantage of the fine bluish film at the back of a very extraordinary *double* nicolo, the front of which is adorned by the antique Omphale, No. 316. The historical interest of the stone is commemorated in the description of that gem.

A Medina gem (Cat. No. 28 M).
Figured in the "Marlborough Gems," Vol. ii. No. 18.

310.—A cameo of renaissance workmanship, the subject being similar to that of No. 295.

An Arundel gem (Cat. Thee. A, No. 142).

311.—A head to the left of the youthful Hercules (*not* Alexander), with the lion's skin head-dress. It is an intaglio of the most beautiful workmanship, and of the purest design, engraved by a Greek artist of the best period, on a fine golden sard.

Once Lord Chesterfield's (Bessborough Cat. No. 6 C).

312.—A head of Omphale to the left (or Iole?); in the garb of Hercules, with the lion's skin head-dress. It is beautifully finished, but the profile is not antique in character, nor is the state of the surface such. It is probably a work of Natter's, a conclusion by no means controverted by the signature it bears of **ΓΝΑΙΟΣ**. It is cut in a yellowish sard of the finest colour and quality.

A Bessborough gem (Cat. No. 43).

313.—The same subject in profile to the left, on a fine hyacinthine sard. Probably a modern work by one of the master hands of the last century.

Once Lord Chesterfield's. A Bessborough gem (Cat. No. 14 C).

56   THE HEROES—HERACLEAN CYCLE.

314.—A full-length intaglio of Omphale in the Herculean lion's skin garb, semi-nude. A beautifully modelled and finished gem, of good Greek work, on a somewhat convex pale amethyst.

    One of the Medina gems in Lord Bessborough's Collection (Cat. No. 7 M).
    Figured in the "Marlborough Gems," Vol. ii. No. 46, and among Worlidge's Etchings, No. 40.

315.—The same subject in intaglio on a golden sard, but less artistically handled; but by a Greek engraver. It is much worn.

316.—An antique cameo, representing a bust to the right of Omphale; in design similar to No. 313. Cut in a double nicolo, of indubitable antiquity, having the original Indian perforation traversing it. At the back is the renaissance cameo of Hercules, No. 309. This gem possesses an historical interest, from its having been presented by Charles V. to Pope Clement VII., and by him subsequently to the Piccolomini of Sienna. It is mounted in a broad gold setting, with eight table diamonds and rubies, alternately, on either face; and between each pair of these stones is a delicate filigree ornament of triplets of trefoil, tied into a sort of golden fleur-de-lis. The edge is ornamented with a twist of vine branches and leaves in black enamel. The setting is of the same period as the gift.

    A Medina gem (Bessb. Cat. No. 28 M).
    Figured by Borioni in the Museum Piccolomini, Plate iii. (No. 45). Also in the "Marlborough Gems," Vol. ii. No. 18.

317.—Omphale, profile to the right, same subject as those previously described. It is a cameo in the style of the third century; the hair is worked in a yellowish surface layer, the face in a stratum of opaque white on a ground of bluish black.

    An Arundel gem (Cat. Thec. B, No. 20).

318.—The same subject to the left; a poor work in cameo of the renaissance period, on an onyx of a singular quality and colour.

    An Arundel gem (Cat. Thec. B, No. 17).

319.—A remarkable cameo in lapis lazuli, representing profile busts to the right of Hercules and Iole, or rather portraits so personified. The appearance of the gem is antique, and especially Græco-Egyptian; the eyes in particular, from their somewhat staring expression, and the line round the iris, seem to indicate this. The portraits may possibly be those of a Ptolemy and his queen, or they may represent personages of importance during the reign of a Ptolemy.

    An Arundel gem (Cat. Thec. C, No. 9).

Leander.

320.—Intaglio head, to the left, of Leander, or the figure called in catalogues Leucothoe (a moon behind the head). Cut in a bold style of Roman workmanship, in a circular red sard, foiled.

A Bessborough gem (Cat. No. 42).

321.—Hero and Leander, intaglio. A work of the renaissance period, on a very fine sard (a sardine), its age being sufficiently indicated by the representation of the Winds.

A Bessborough gem (Cat. No. 85).

322.—Leander. A bust to the left, as though swimming, cut in intaglio on a sard; perhaps of Roman work.

An Arundel gem (Cat. Thec. A, No. 28), termed "Caput Athletæ."

Meleager.

323.—A very fine sard, with a figure of a huntsman carrying a spear, probably Meleager; cut in intaglio, in a somewhat slight manner: apparently an antique work, but the modelling is inferior.

A Bessborough gem, termed Adonis (Cat. No. 32 c).

324.—A modern work in intaglio, on a sard, called by Natter, in his Catalogue of the Bessborough Gems, a "Meleager."

(Bessb. Cat. No. 97).

325.—A beautiful bit of minute Italian renaissance work, comprising 27 figures, and styled "The death of Meleager." It is cut in shallow cameo on the top of a shell of Cypræa tigris.

An Arundel gem (Cat. Thec. C, No. 18).

Amazons.

326.—A cameo of rare beauty and in the finest antique work. An Amazon, whose helmet is cut in a little boss of transparent red sard, supports her dead comrade whose horse stands by looking towards the distant conflict. The figures are cut out of an ivory-white layer upon a fine brownish sard base.

Figured in the "Marlborough Gems," Vol. i. No. 48.

327.—A cameo, representing an Amazon unhorsed, and seized by a warrior. (Theseus and Antiope.) The stone is a sardonyx, so cut that the Amazon is represented in a surface layer of opaque white, the horse and the warrior in a horn-like stratum, on a base of chalcedony. The work belongs to the best Roman period.

Bellerophon, and Pegasus.

328.—Bellerophon and Pegasus, a chimæra below; a late Roman intaglio engraved on a nicolo.

An Arundel gem (Cat. Thec. A, No. 64).

329.—Bellerophon watering Pegasus at the Hippocrene. An intaglio cut in a rich shaded sard. The figure of the Bellerophon looks antique, but the horse and background, in which a name is inscribed, hardly corroborate it. The name may be read as **ΟΤΙΑΤΟΥ, ΟΠΑΤΟΥ** or **ΟΤΙΛΤΟΥ**. Without doubt a copy from, if it be not the gem with the same subject described by Raspe as lettered **ΣΩΤΡΑΤΟΥ**, which was, according to Dr. Brunn, a modern copy from the bas relief with this subject in the Palazzo Spada. A similar gem is in the Berlin Collection, but without the name, and there are other copies in existence.

[Pegasus.]

330.—The fore quarters and wing of Pegasus beautifully engraved in intaglio in a hyacinth. The curl of the wing is in the most authentically antique manner, like that on coins of Lampsacus or of Corinth.

Theseus.

331.—Theseus, having slain the Minotaur, rests on his club; the dead monster lies in a window of the Labyrinth : a very pretty modern cameo cut in a porcelain-white layer in relief, on a bluish-grey base; perhaps by the hand of Natter, who figured this subject in his work on gem engraving. The same subject occurs on a gem at Vienna, confessedly modern, and signed Philemon.

Heroes of the Trojan War.

332.—Priam at the feet of Achilles. A beautiful little Greek intaglio on a fine sard. Four figures are included in the design, of which the finish is complete, even to the ornamentation of the cuirass of Achilles.

One of the Medina gems (Bessb. Cat. No. 44 M).

333.—A seated warrior, in intaglio (called in the Blenheim Catalogue an Achilles), contemplates a helmet. The gem exhibits a roughness of outline and imperfection in the drawing which condemn it as a forgery of the last century. It is engraved on a beautiful little sard.

334.—An intaglio; a crouching warrior (the so-called wounded Achilles—perhaps Tydeus); a round buckler covers his side with a Gorgon head on it, and his sword is erect in his hand before him. It is cut deeply into a good pale sard in an antique style.

335.—A cameo, Roman in date, on sardonyx. Achilles or a hero holding forth a sword. He is seated on a cuirass. It is cut in a white layer, with a brown base layer.

An Arundel gem (Cat. Thec. A, 140).

336.—An intaglio; Thetis borne on a Triton conveying the arms to her son. Late Roman work; deeply and rudely cut in a red cornelian.

337.—Head of Diomed; a cameo, with the character of a late Roman work, cut in a sardonyx out of a white layer on a base of sard.

One of the Medina gems (Bessb. Cat. No. 40 M).

338.—Achilles and Chiron. The Centaur is giving the young Achilles a lesson on the lyre; a Cupid behind is listening. Perhaps a work of the 2nd century: it is deeply cut in intaglio on a fine sard, but the subject is so treated in a picture found at Pompeii, possibly the original from which this gem may have been copied by a modern hand. There are many modern copies of the same design.

THE HEROES—HEROES OF THE ILIAD CYCLE.

339.—An intaglio of Achilles and a Centaur; rather late Roman work, as seen by its rudeness and by the material in which it is engraved, a red jasper.

One of the Chesterfield gems acquired by Lord Bessborough (Cat. No. 31 c).

340.—Two figures engraved in intaglio on a very fine and large yellow sard, representing, perhaps, Paris and Œnone. The figures are nude, and are not therefore (as the Blenheim Catalogue interprets them) Phaon and Sappho. The gem has been very much rubbed down by modern polishing, but is fine work, and likely to have been cut by an antique hand.

Mr. King considers the figures to represent a muse and comic poet.

The gem was once Mariette's; see Caylus, Rec. 1, p. 129.

340a.—An intaglio, that seems to be a modern copy on a reduced scale of the Paris and Œnone, No. 340; stated by a note in the Duke of Marlborough's handwriting to have been engraved by Natter. It is cut on quartz.

341.—An intaglio on a deep-coloured sard (or sardine), of the large dimensions of $1\frac{3}{4}$ inch by $1\frac{1}{16}$ inch. It represents Diomed and Ulysses seizing the Palladium. Diomed on one side is seated on a cippus, in the attitude so often repeated upon gems, holding the talismanic image in his left, and his sword in his right hand (as viewed on an impression). On the other, the left half of the stone (the right on an impression from it), Ulysses, the herald's staff in his left hand and the chlamys on his other arm, points to the body of the priestess at his feet. A figure with a trident (of Poseidon?) surmounts a tall column that divides the gem and separates the two heroes; while the wall of the temple-precinct is seen over Ulysses' head.

On the cippus is the signature ΦΗΛΙΞ ΕΠΟΙΕΙ, and in the field over the head of Diomed, as if to balance in the design the wall on the other side, are the words ΚΑΛΠΟΥΡΝΙΟΥ ϹΕΟΥΗΡΟΥ, the name, perhaps, of the owner. This important and remarkable gem is one of the very few that the scepticism of Stephani allowed as carrying a genuine signature. Dr. Brunn, while admitting this verdict (in opposition to the opinions of Bracci and of Kohler), has been, with Stephani, misled as to the position of the inscriptions; perhaps in consequence of the engraving, No. XXXV. in Stosch's work, having the whole of the inscriptions consecutively in the exergue. Worlidge has made no such error. The Arundel sardine—or dark sard (not a sardonyx, by the way, for which

THE HEROES—HEROES OF THE ILIAD CYCLE.

the *sardoine* has been mistaken,)—has had a suspicious look imparted to it by a vigorous re-polishing (too usual in the Arundel gems), and by probably a considerable thinning of the stone, the back being worked down to show the quality of the sardine. The position of this intaglio in this Collection as an Arundelian gem secures it at least from the charge of being a forgery of the last century. There are certainly points about it calculated to awaken suspicion as to its antiquity; such as the form of the figure of Neptune on the column, and a certain appearance as of a simulated early style in the treatment of parts. But the form of the owner's name is hardly such as would have been forged before the last century; and there seems no valid ground for withholding from this remarkable intaglio the title Brunn has allowed to it of ancient workmanship. It was probably a work of the age of Hadrian.

An Arundel gem (Ar. Cat. Thec. E, No. 2).
Figured in the "Marlborough Gems," Vol. i. No. 39, and by Worlidge in his Etchings, No. 52, where he has put the inscriptions in their correct positions.

342.—Intaglio; Diomed, master of the Palladium; a renaissance work of very inferior style, on an agate.

An Arundel gem (Cat. Thec. E, No. 9).

343.—A gem in intaglio with the singular lettering **ΔΙΟΓΗΝΕΣ**. The dress is that of Ulysses,—the pilos and chiton. The work is apparently of a pretty good Roman period of art, on a nicolo. But the name seems certainly to have been engraved at a date subsequent to that of the intaglio. Besides the inversion of the H and E, the dress would prove the figure not to be the philosophic wearer of one single rag, though the (pithos) earthen pot, on which the crouching figure is seated, might represent his tub.

Æneas.

344.—An intaglio of Apollo helping Æneas (who is only represented by his last retreating leg) to escape from Diomed through the Scæan gate : Diomed is striking at a cloud unrepresented in the gem.

It is a fine work, cut in a rich and uniform sard, square in form with the angles rounded, and set in a light and beautiful ring of 17*th century workmanship*. Winckelmann described a similar work on an "antique" paste. Natter gave his opinion in favour of the antiquity of this gem, but declared the paste alluded to to have been a modern one made from it. The surface of the work on the wall, however, makes the antiquity of the gem itself rather doubtful.

>It was from the Medina Collection (Bessb. Cat. No. 21 M). It seems to have belonged to Caylus in 1762. See his Thec. d'Antiquités, V., Pl. liii. 3.
>Figured by Worlidge, No. 17, and in the "Marlborough Gems," Vol. i. No. 46.

344 *bis.* Diomed and Æneas at the Scæan gate : the same subject as the last, but cut in cameo on a good sardonyx. It is inscribed **YΔPOY**, Natter's punning pseudonym, (natter being in German a water-snake).

>Natter figured and described the last gem, No. 344, in his Treatise. No doubt he copied all the gems he has there described.

345.—Æneas carrying Anchises, and conducting Ascanius. An intaglio worked during the good Roman period, on a fine pale sard.

346.—Two warriors conversing, Pylades and Orestes ? An intaglio on a foiled sard, and probably a renaissance work. Mr. King terms them Achilles and Antilochus, and considers the work as late Greek.

>An Arundel gem (Cat. Thec. A, No. 62).

347.—An intaglio ; Tydeus with the head of Melanippus. An Etruscan or early Greek work on a sard. On the reverse is a Victory.

>A Bessborough gem (Cat. No. 52).

348.—Iphigenia or Polyxena, offered in sacrifice ; a rude Roman intaglio on a sard.

>An Arundel gem (Cat. Thec. A, No. 79).

349.—A full-faced head of Laocoon, cut on a rich amethyst in cameo in the last century. It was, in fact, engraved by Sirletti, according to Mariette.

>A Bessborough gem (Cat. No. 21).
>Figured in the "Marlborough Gems," Vol. i. No. 25.

350.—A very fine shell cameo of Laocoon. The drawing and design are admirable, and the work probably of the 17th century, perhaps even by the hand of Fiamingo.

II.—ICONOGRAPHY.

1.—*GREEK AND PRE-AUGUSTAN PORTRAITURE.*

351.—An intaglio head of Homer to the right. A beautiful and delicate Greek work, on a fine yellow sard, representing the conventional features of the poet.

352.—A very small cameo; a head to the right representing Sappho; very like in profile and head-dress to the Sappho heads on the small electrum coins of Lesbos. It is cut in a white layer on a reddish base, and is probably Greek work.

One of the Medina gems in the Bessborough Collection (Cat. No. 10 M).

353.—Intaglio on a plasma. A female head to the left tied with ribbons in a style usually attributed to Sappho.

One of the gems originally Lord Chesterfield's (Bessb. Cat. No. 24 c).

354.—An intaglio head, to the right, of Socrates, on dark jasper. Fine work, probably of the early Imperial time.

355.—A poor Roman intaglio on a cornelian; a head to the right that seems meant for Socrates.

356.—An intaglio; Socrates and Plato, on a fine almandine garnet, being a representation of the heads of the two philosophers, confronting one another. A precise duplicate of this fine gem on a poor cornelian is in the Bibliothèque Impériale at Paris. Both gems have all the appearance of being Greco-Roman work, of the early Imperial age. This cabochon almandine belonged to the Earl of Chesterfield before falling into the Bessborough Collection. It can hardly have been a copy from the gem at Paris. Both were probably ancient works from a common original.

(Bessb. Cat. No. 7 c.) Figured by Worlidge, 33, and in "Marlborough Gems," Vol. ii. No. 3.

GREEK AND PRE-AUGUSTAN PORTRAITURE.

357.—An intaglio, head of Plato, on a fine brown sard, to the left; fine Roman work.

358.—Cameo head of Alexander the Great, to the right. The helmet is ornamented in very low relief by a combat between one warrior and another in a chariot (?) drawn by gryphons. The whole work is perhaps of the renaissance period, or the ornaments on the helmet, as Mr. King suggests, may have been superposed upon work which, if Roman, must have belonged to the earlier Imperial times. If an ancient work, it probably was wrought in its entirety in the time of Caracalla or of Severus Alexander. The stone is a fine sardonyx, of which a clear white layer forms the face, in relief upon a black ground; a surface layer of a red coral colour forming the helmet.

An Arundel gem (Cat. Thec. C, No. 5).
Figured in the "Marlborough Gems," Vol. ii. No. 4.

359.—A modern but beautiful little cameo, representing Alexander the Great. The face, to the right, is in an opaque white layer on a base of horny chalcedony.

360.—The same subject, to the right, with Pichler's signature, ΠΙΧΛΕΡ. This cameo is on a fine sardonyx; the Ammon horn standing out in a surface layer of a rich brown colour.

361.—A small cameo, carrying what is probably meant to be a bust, to the right, of Alexander. The work is pretty good, but not antique.

362.—A helmeted head of rather deep intaglio, three-quarter face, of the type usually called "Hannibal." It might be rather late Italo-Greek work. It is on a good sard, and is a beautiful gem, but its date is uncertain, from the numerous repetitions of the subject by excellent artists.

363.—Same subject cut in intaglio on a large agate, either a renaissance work, or of the last century.

A Bessborough gem (Cat. No. 35).
Etched by Worlidge, No. 16, and figured in the "Marlborough Gems," Vol. ii. No. 20.

364.—An admirable portrait of Demetrius III., Philopator. It is in the style of the contemporary Greek work, being cut in a shallow manner on a sard; the head to the right.

Figured by Worlidge, in his Etchings, as a Tiberius.

365.—A small cameo probably modern, apparently intended for the last of the Ptolemies. The hair is in a yellow and dark brown layer; the face, which is to the right, is in white, on a greyish translucent base. It is set in an open mounting of silver with small diamonds.

366.—An Egyptian queen in the vulture head-dress, as a priestess of Isis; called a Cleopatra. The face and head, to the left, are cut in a rich brown layer of sard on a white base. The work is of a grand and bold order, but not highly finished, though admirable in polish. This cameo is probably the Ptolemaic-Greek original of many copies.

<blockquote>
It was from the Bessborough Collection (Cat. No. 2), and called an Isis.

Figured in the "Marlborough Gems," Vol. ii. No. 17.
</blockquote>

367.—A modern cameo, probably by a French artist, representing a bust of Cleopatra full-faced, and in the conventional modern type; on an onyx.

2.—ROMAN AND POST-AUGUSTAN PORTRAITURE.

368.—A modern intaglio on a sard, meant perhaps to represent Lucius Junius Brutus; a head to the left.

<blockquote>
One of the Chesterfield gems (Cat. No. 21 c, "Metrodorus").

Figured in the "Marlborough Gems," Vol. ii. No. 2, as Metrodorus, and also by Worlidge, No. 34.
</blockquote>

369.—The same subject, to the left, an intaglio, cut in a convex sard. Work of the last century, or renaissance, roughened to give it an ancient appearance.

<blockquote>
Perhaps an Arundel gem (Ar. Cat. Thec. A, 11).
</blockquote>

370.—An intaglio of renaissance work on a bright red sard. A helmeted head in three-quarter face with the lettering M. RE. ATI., and intended to represent Marcus Atilius Regulus.

<blockquote>
An Arundel gem (Cat. Thec. A, 12).
</blockquote>

371.—An intaglio of the same age as the last, on a sard, lettered COS VII, and meant for Caius Marius; the head to the right.

<blockquote>
An Arundel gem (Cat. Thec. A, No. 10).
</blockquote>

66 ROMAN AND POST-AUGUSTAN PORTRAITURE.

372.—A renaissance or modern intaglio on a fine little sapphire, representing Cicero; the head to the left.

From the Chesterfield Collection (Bessb. Cat. No. 11 c).

373.—An intaglio on red jasper of rather nice work, doubtless representing a portrait of Sextus Pompeius; the head to the left.

A Bessborough gem (Cat. No. 53), termed Ptolemy the Great.

374.—An intaglio of good Roman work, meant probably for Sextus Pompeius, though neither this nor the previous portrait are much like that on his rare gold coin; the head is to the left, on a sard.

An Arundel gem (Cat. Thec. A, No. 13).

375.—A portrait in profile, to the left, of Marcus Junius Brutus. It is a beautifully worked intaglio on a rich little sard. The form of the head is somewhat different from that represented on the coins, but it is without doubt intended for his portrait, and it is certainly Roman work not later than the early Imperial time.

From the Chesterfield Collection (Bessb. Cat. No. 3 c).
Figured in the "Marlborough Gems," Vol. i. No. 4, and by Worlidge, No. 10.

376.—The above copied on a beautiful sard in modern times; interesting from the contrast the work affords to its antique prototype.

From the Bessborough Collection (Cat. No. 55).

377.—An intaglio on a very fine nicolo, probably representing Lucius Junius Brutus; a head to the left, by a renaissance hand.

An Arundel gem (Thec. A, No. 146).

378.—Mark Antony; an intaglio on a fine golden sard. The face, to the right, is somewhat less hard in feature than on coins, and thus bears some resemblance to Vespasian. It seems a contemporary work, and in the finest manner of the Græco-Roman period.

379.—An intaglio, probably of Lepidus, on a bright red sard; good work, probably of the early Imperial age; the head to the left.

380.—A head, to the left, of Julius Cæsar on a nicolo; an intaglio of little character, and probably modern.

381.—An intaglio. The same subject with still less of the character of Julius Cæsar. A renaissance work, only remarkable for the stone that it is upon—a sapphire; the head is to the left.

An Arundel gem (Cat. Thec. A, No. 15).

382.—Intaglio. The same head, to the left, in very exaggerated style, probably of the cinque-cento period, on a magnificent nicolo.

A Bessborough gem (Cat. No. 19).
Figured in the "Marlborough Gems," Vol. i. No. 3.

383.—A portrait, probably meant for Julius Cæsar, or it might even be commemorative of William III. of England. A rather nice modern intaglio, the head to the right, on a sapphire.

One of the Bessborough gems (Cat. No. 48).

384.—An intaglio head, probably meant for Julius Cæsar, coarsely engraved in a large but poor sard by some cinque-cento hand; the head to the left.

An Arundel gem (Cat. Thec. E, No. 12).

385.—A small statuette bust, cut out of a magnificent hyacinthine sard, as beautiful for colour as for transparency. It is called Nerva, but is probably meant for Julius Cæsar, and would seem to be a work of the fine period of the cinque-cento.

It was an Arundel gem (Cat. Thec. C, No. 16).
Figured in the "Marlborough Gems," Vol. i. No. 17.

386.—Intaglio of Augustus very young; a head to the left. Good but not very fine Roman work, on a hyacinthine sard.

A Bessborough gem (Cat. No. 2 c).
Figured by Worlidge and in the "Marlborough Gems," Vol. i. No. 6, and called there a Lepidus.

387.—A fragment, being part of a portrait of Augustus, to the left, in the character of Hermes, a caduceus being in the field; in shallow intaglio. When complete it must have been some 3 inches high by nearly 2 inches broad. It is cut in a brown sard, and delicately finished. It is difficult to assign a date to this gem: but see No. 122, which is a gem very similar in style.

This gem seems to have been one of those acquired by the third Duke, and is figured in the "Marlborough Gems," Vol. ii. No. 16.
It is probably the fragment alluded to in a letter from Marchant to his Grace, and for which 23 guineas was paid. See Introduction, p. xvii.

68   ROMAN AND POST-AUGUSTAN PORTRAITURE.

388.—A modern intaglio of considerable merit, on a sard, representing Augustus in apotheosis; the head to the left, no doubt studied from the large brass coins.

389.—A modern and fine cameo, in a splendid nicolo, of a head of Augustus. A rim is reserved, formed in the upper bluish layer of the stone.

390.—A cameo, nearly three inches in height. Head, looking to the right, of the deified Augustus (with the radiate crown); extremely fine work. The emperor's head is left in a porcelain-white layer in relief, on a reddish brown sard under layer; altogether a noble gem of the period of the early empire. The setting of this cameo is beautifully chiselled and elaborately enamelled; wrought probably in the cinque-cento period.

Figured in the "Marlborough Gems," Vol. i. No. 7.

391.—A cameo, representing probably Augustus deified. The head is seen in front face, veiled, and in the highest relief. It is cut in an opaque white porcelain-like layer, but the ground has been fractured, cut off, and substituted by gold. It is a noble Roman work, 1¾ inch high by 1 inch in width.

From the Bessborough Collection (Cat. No. 3).
Figured in the "Marlborough Gems," Vol. i. No. 8.

392.—A cameo, in very high relief, apparently representing Augustus when young, crowned with a laurel wreath. It is very beautiful work, but of comparatively modern, though uncertain, date. The features are carved in a fine porcelain-white stratum of an onyx, 1½ inch high by 1 inch wide; the base is brown.

From the Bessborough Collection (Cat. No. 4).
Figured in the "Marlborough Gems," Vol. i. No. 12, as Germanicus.

393.—A small, quite modern cameo on sardonyx, representing the head of young Augustus, looking to the left, in a white layer on a brown ground.

394.—A much worn, and possibly antique cameo, representing the same subject as the last, looking to the right; cut in an opaque yellow layer of an onyx with a bluish-gray base.

395.—A cameo of renaissance period, representing Augustus laureated, in a clear amethystine chalcedony with an opaline foil, and mounted in white enamel, adorned with flowers; a portrait to the right.

An Arundel gem (Cat. Thec. B, No. 21).

396.—A fine modern cameo, probably representing the head of Augustus to the left, in a pale coffee-tinted layer, on a dark bluish-gray base.

396a.—A very fine modern cameo, in high relief, nearly front-faced bust, probably also of Augustus, in an opaque white layer, on a pinkish-grey ground.

397.—A modern paste cameo, white on black ground, perhaps also meant for Augustus; the head to the left.

398.—A modern cameo of beautiful workmanship, representing a profile head of Augustus to the left, cut on a whitish layer on a bluish base.

399.—A profile and bust to the right, representing Livia. It is a small cameo, of Roman workmanship, on a sardonyx.

400.—A minute cameo; a small female veiled head to the right, cut on a sardonyx, the face in a white layer, the veil in a yellow surface layer, on a base of jet black. It is good, probably Roman work, and may represent Livia; mounted in a tasteful blue enamelled ring, adorned with stars.

An Arundel gem (Cat. Thec. A, No. 109).

401.—A bust of Livia veiled, and in front face, represented as Ceres. A cameo on a sardonyx, in very high relief, carved in a porcelain-white layer, on a mottled sard base. The gem is 1¾ inch in height.

An Arundel gem (Cat. Thec. C, No. 7).
Figured in the "Marlborough Gems," Vol. ii. 24.

402.—A female head and part of bust to the left; possibly Livia, in the character of Ceres. A cameo, on a sardonyx, the hair and veil in a jet-black layer; the face in a white stratum, with the base layer black. It may be a Ceres, however, of the age of Severus; the work being of the rude type then prevalent. It is prettily set, like 446, in a gold wire looped border.

Perhaps the Arundel gem (Cat. Thec. A, No. 124).

ROMAN AND POST-AUGUSTAN PORTRAITURE.

403.—A cameo of extraordinary beauty and interest; Livia and the young Tiberius, in green turquoise. The work as perfect as the stone is remarkable. It is without doubt a gem of the Augustan age, and may once have been a much larger composition, and constructed in pieces, of which this was one. It is 1¼ inch in height by 1½ inch in width.

<small>It was in the Bessborough Collection (Cat. p. 27).
It is exquisitely figured in the "Marlborough Gems," Vol. i. No. 10.</small>

404.—An intaglio head, to the left, on cornelian; very good work, probably meant for the young Tiberius.

405.—A cameo head, cut in a white layer on a yellow sard ground, apparently meant for Tiberius. The portrait looks to the left, and has the character of a modern work.

<small>An Arundel gem (Cat. Thec. A, No. 108), termed Drusus son of Tiberius.
Figured in the "Marlborough Gems," Vol. ii. No. 25.</small>

406.—A cameo, 1¼ inch in height, by nearly 1 inch in width. A bust of the young Tiberius to the left; the face rendered in a white layer, the wreath and shoulder in a yellow brown layer, on a base of mottled yellow chalcedony. Fine Roman work; the likeness injured by an abrasion of the nose.

<small>From the Bessborough Collection (Cat. No. 6).</small>

407.—A cameo, 3 inches in height by 1¾ in width, probably meant to represent Tiberius, the portrait being much like his coins struck in Asia Minor. The work, however, is rude, and may belong to a later period. The face, a portrait to the right, is cut in a bluish-white layer, on a translucent base of yellowish chalcedony.

408.—A minute cameo; a head to the left, in a yellowish layer of a sardonyx, with a grey base. It probably represents Marcus Agrippa, and would seem to be contemporary work.

409.—The same subject with the rostral crown, but perhaps modern; the portrait is to the left, in a white layer of an onyx on a translucent base.

<small>Figured in the "Marlborough Gems," Vol. ii. No. 23.</small>

410.—A large bloodstone cameo, 3 inches high, by 2½ in width. A head to the left, intended for Agrippa. It is probably a modern work.

411.—A "Marcellus," so called, copied by Marchant in intaglio, on a wonderfully fine hyacinthine garnet, from the cameo No. 412. The head is to the right.

412.—A cameo; a head in a white layer, on a gray ground, looking to the left; perhaps meant for Marcellus, but doubtful both in its age and subject.

> An Arundel gem (Cat. Thec. A, No. 116).
> Figured in the "Marlborough Gems," Vol. i. No. 9, as Marcellus.

413.—A cameo portrait in shallow relief to the left, in a white layer on a black base. A renaissance work, intended for Drusus.

> Apparently the Arundel gem (Cat. Thec. A, No. 120).
> Figured in the "Marlborough Gems," Vol. i. No. 11.

414.—A cameo on a sardonyx, 1¼ inch high, by 1½ inch wide. A fine laureated head to the right; the laurel wreath and robe in a rich yellow layer; flesh in a pure white layer, on a ground of yellowish brown. Possibly intended for Antonia, but the likeness is not very strong. It is, however, good Roman work of the Imperial age.

> An Arundel gem (Cat. Thec. C, No. 2).
> Figured in the "Marlborough Gems," Vol. ii. No. 27.

415.—Conjoined heads of Germanicus and Agrippina to the left. Poor cinque-cento work on an onyx, cut in a white layer on a bluish-gray base.

> An Arundel gem (Cat. Thec. B, No. 3).

416.—Cameo on a sardonyx, 1½ inch in height, by 1¼ inch in width. A head of Agrippina the elder to the right. The richly worked hair and laurel wreath is cut in a fine brown layer; the face in a bluish-white stratum, on a dark base. The work is very fine, and worthy of the magnificent stone on which it is cut. It is a noble gem of the Augustan age. It is mounted in an enamelled black and gold setting.

> An Arundel gem (Cat. Thec. D, No. 2).

417.—An intaglio portrait of Agrippina, the younger, to the left, lightly veiled as Ceres, on a splendid red sard, an inch in height. It is a modern gem, with the assumed signature **ΑCΠΑCΙΟΥ**, attributed by Bracci to Flavio Sirletti.

> One of the Medina gems (Bessb. Cat. No. 14 M).
> Figured by Worlidge, and in the "Marlborough Gems," Vol. i. No. 14.

418.—A copy, signed by Pichler, from the sitting statue of Agrippina in the Villa Albani. A pretty cameo.

419.—Cameo, entirely in sard : a head of Caius Cæsar. Excellent and antique work, set in a brass ring.

An Arundel gem (Cat. Thec. A, No. 110).

420.—An intaglio portrait to the left, on a beryl or pale sapphire ; probably meant for the young Caligula. It is set in a fine massive mediæval ring.

An Arundel gem (Cat. Thec. C, No. 17).

421.—A renaissance cameo, representing Caligula ; a head to the left, in a black layer on a grayish-brown ground.

An Arundel gem (Ar. Cat. Thec. B, No. 19).

422.—A cameo, representing Claudius Cæsar to the left, with an oaken crown and the paludamentum. It is cut on a sardonyx, $2\frac{7}{8}$ inches high, by 2 inches wide, and set in a finely enamelled mounting. The flesh is rendered in a porcelain-white layer, the wreath and ægis in a reserved stratum of fine yellow, while the base is also composed of yellow sard. The work is rather coarse, and probably contemporary. It is set in a rim of enamelled gold.

An Arundel gem, termed Britannicus (Ar. Cat. Thec. D, No. 9).

423.—A cameo bust of Claudius to the right, on a fine sardonyx, $2\frac{1}{8}$ inches high, by $1\frac{3}{4}$ inch wide ; the face being cut in a translucent bluish-white layer, the hair in a whiter stratum, the civic oak wreath and the paludamentum in a rich brown sard layer, and the base consisting of tortoise shell sard. The work is much the same quality as that in No. 422, and seems to be contemporary with the emperor. It is set in a rim of plain gold.

An Arundel gem (Cat. Thec. C, No. 11).

424.—A small front-face portrait of Messalina in cameo, in high relief, on a weathered lapis lazuli. The work is good, and perhaps contemporary.

425.—An intaglio portrait of Nero to the left, at about twenty-four years of age, on a fragment of sard. The likeness is fairly good, and the work contemporary ; at least that portion of the gem which has not been added to complete the subject.

An Arundel gem (Cat. Thec. A, No. 18).

ROMAN AND POST-AUGUSTAN PORTRAITURE.

426.—A small cameo head of Nero to the left. Contemporary, and not very good work. The head in a white layer on a grayish-black ground.

An Arundel gem (Cat. Thec. A, No. 107).

427.—Cameo, 1¾ inch high by 1 inch wide, carrying a head of Nero to the left; cut in a wax-like pinkish layer in middle relief, on a somewhat yellow opaque base. It is fine work, and probably contemporary.

428.—A small renaissance cameo, representing a head of Nero to the right; in a white layer on a gray ground.

429.—A small onyx cameo, head of Nero to the right. Of dubious but probably cinque-cento date, in a white layer on a gray ground.

430.—A small cameo on sardonyx, with the same subject to the left; in a yellow-brown layer on a white base. It seems a renaissance work.

An Arundel gem (Cat. Thec. B, No. 27).

431.—Small cameo, on a garnet foiled so as to have the appearance of an amethyst; perhaps Nero, but possibly Domitian, and described as such in the Arundel Catalogue, on a garnet. It seems a modern or renaissance work.

An Arundel gem (Cat. Thec. A, No. 115)?—described as on a garnet.

432.—Onyx; small cameo, head of Nero to the left, in a white layer on a gray ground: probably modern.

433.—Sardonyx; a very fine cameo, representing the laureated head of Galba to the left, being a fragment of a larger gem. It is 1½ inch high by 1 inch wide, in a marble white layer, on a black base. It seems ancient but reworked in later times.

An Arundel gem (Cat. Thec. A, No. 123).
Figured in the " Marlborough Gems," Vol. i. No. 16.

434.—Onyx; a small cameo head of Galba to the right. Probably contemporary; in a white layer on a bluish-gray base.

An Arundel gem (Cat. Thec. A, No. 117).

435.—Onyx; a small cameo, ⅜ths of an inch high, representing, perhaps, Galba, or it may be Vespasian, to the right. A finely worked little gem: the face cut in a dead white layer on a black base.

436.—An extraordinary sardonyx, $3\frac{1}{2}$ inches high by $2\frac{7}{8}$ inches wide, with a helmeted head and bust upon it, in rather low relief. The base of the stone consists of deep red, almost black sard; the face and crest of the helmet and neck are worked in a white layer, while the helmet and coat of mail are reserved in an upper layer of deep brown hue. The subject, a bust to the right, with a helmet and coat of what may be intended as chain armour, has been described as Galba. Round the head has been written in characters not engraved, but stained into the stone, the words: ANDREAS CARRAIA SANCTA COMES SOVERINAL:—"André de St. Carée, Count of Soverinal." This lettering can be seen by strong sun light, or by breathing on the stone, and illustrates the singular porosity that characterises chalcedony, even in the form of the finest sard. It is perhaps the name of some owner of the gem; or it might even be the personage pourtrayed upon it. That it is not a work of antique time may be assumed from the nature of the stone, which is like those from the neighbourhood of Oberstein, and is artificially coloured; probably at that place. The onyxes so stained in Germany are of a softer and more porous kind than the sard varieties chiefly employed by the ancients, which, when altered in colour, were generally changed by the action of heat only.

This splendid sardonyx was in the Bessborough Collection (Cat. No. 15).

437.—An onyx cameo representing Galba to the right; a very nice work of the cinque-cento period; cut on a stone $1\frac{1}{2}$ inch in height in a white stratum on a horn-like base.

An Arundel gem (Cat. Thec. B, No. 40).
Figured in the "Marlborough Gems," Vol. i. No. 16.

438.—Onyx cameo; a small renaissance head, probably meant for Galba to the left.

439.—Onyx cameo; head of Otho, in a white layer on a dark gray ground, probably a renaissance gem.

An Arundel gem (Cat. Thec. A, No. 118).

440.—Yellowish chalcedony; a small intaglio head of Vespasian to the left, but not much like that emperor, and may, perhaps, be intended for Galba. It is mounted in a very pretty ring.

An Arundel gem (Cat. Thec. A, No. 19).

441.—Red jasper; head of Vespasian to the left. A somewhat flattered portrait, apparently of his time.

442.—Small cameo on onyx; a head of Vespasian to the right, in a white layer on a dark base. Rude contemporary work.

An Arundel gem (Cat. Thec. A, No. 121).

443.—Sardonyx; a small cinque-cento cameo, mounted in a very pretty ring, representing Vespasian to the right, in a white layer on a bluish-gray ground, with laurel wreath in a yellow layer, and a rim in the white layer.

An Arundel gem (Cat. Thec. A, No. 106).

444.—Onyx; a stone $1\frac{3}{5}$ inch high by $1\frac{1}{2}$ inch wide. A three-quarter face head of Vespasian; against a flesh-coloured under layer the face is seen in white with a slight tint of flesh colour. The expression is slightly exaggerated, and the work, which is very good, is probably modern; as indeed is the stone, a German onyx.

445.—An intaglio on a large plasma, $1\frac{1}{4}$ inch high by $\frac{7}{8}$ths inch wide. Head of Titus to the right. The expression is not good, and the work is probably renaissance.

An Arundel gem (Cat. Thec. E, No. 20).

446.—Sardonyx; a cameo representing probably the head of Titus to the left, taken from his Alexandrian coins, in a bluish-white translucent layer, and reserved rim on a yellowish-brown base. The work seems to be of the renaissance, and is enclosed in a beautiful gold wire setting, similar to that of No. 402, and in style resembling those of No. 452 and 461.

An Arundel gem (Cat. Thec. A, No. 125), called Vespasian.

447.—An intaglio on a splendid hyacinthine sard. The renowned bust of daughter of Titus by Nicander, whereof the upper part of the head and the head-dress are restored in gold. Mr. King considers it to be a Berenice, but the comparison with coins seems to justify the original attribution. The inscription is beyond all suspicion genuine, and might be of Ptolemaic date. It is retrograde.

NIKANΔP•<
ΕΠ•ΕΙ

The portrait is to the left, and the signature behind the neck. The original height of the gem must have been $1\frac{1}{8}$ inch, its width $\frac{7}{8}$ths nearly. The work is bold, and doubtless contemporary with the personage it represents.

It was formerly in the Deringh Collection.

76 ROMAN AND POST-AUGUSTAN PORTRAITURE.

448.—Intaglio on a sard. A head, to the left, of Domitian when very young. Probably a contemporary work.

 A Bessborough gem (Cat. No. 107).

449.—A cameo on an onyx, representing Domitian to the right. Hard in design, but with the fine workmanship of the cinquecento period. The relief is cut in a white porcelain-like layer on a pale base.

450.—A beautiful plasma. An intaglio to the left, of uncertain but probably modern date, representing, it would seem, Domitia Longina the wife of Domitian, although in some of the features it more resembles Julia Titus' daughter.

 Bought by the third Duke from the jeweller Lavocat for 5l. 5s.

451.—Onyx; a minute renaissance cameo, representing Domitian, to the right; in a white layer on a dark gray ground.

 An Arundel gem (Ar. Cat. Thec. B, No. 24).

452.—Sardonyx; 1⅝ inch high by 1⅜ inch wide. A cameo bust to the left, of probably Trajan senior; dressed with the cuirass carrying the Gorgoneion, perhaps in the garb of a general. In rather flat relief, cut in a white layer over a light brown stratum of the stone. It is set in a gold wire setting with a row of garnets.

 Figured in the "Marlborough Gems," Vol. ii. No. 21, as Sulla.
 An Arundel gem (Ar. Cat. Thec. C, No. 13), termed Gordian, jun.

453.—A paste copy of No. 454.

454.—Intaglio head, to the left, of Sabina or possibly Marciana, on a rich sard. A fine work, probably contemporary.

 From the Chesterfield Collection (Bessb. Cat. No. 1 c), called by Natter, Plotina or Marciana.
 Figured in the "Marlborough Gems," Vol. i, No. 19, as Marciana.

455.—On a fine red sard. An intaglio head of Sabina to the right. Very fine contemporary work.

 Figured in the "Marlborough Gems," Vol. i. No. 20, and etched by Worlidge. See Introduction, p. xvii.

456.—On a fine yellow sard. A head of Sabina in intaglio, by Burch.

457.—On a mottled yellowish chalcedony. A full-faced representation, carved in the round, of Marciana, the sister of Trajan, in apotheosis. This important gem, the dimensions of which are 3 inches in height and width, represents the empress in bust, as if seated on the peacock, which, however, has been much mutilated. This gem, which must have been a work of Trajan's age, was once in the collection of the dukes of Mantua.

A Medina gem, called by Natter, in the Catalogue of the Bessborough gems (Cat. No. 37 M), Domitia. It is figured under this name, too, in the "Marlborough Gems," Vol. ii. No. 28. Domitia, however, died after her husband, and in private life, and could hardly have been thus canonized. Marciana, on the other hand, received the honours of the apotheosis, as coins of the *consecratio* exist.

458.—Intaglio on a garnet. Head of Hadrian to the left. Apparently a good contemporary work.

459.—On a sardonyx. A small bust, apparently of the young Hadrian, to the left, with a coarse imitation of an Etruscan border round it. The intaglio, which appears to be poor Roman work, is cut in a brown layer, below which there is a white layer resting on a black base, the stone being bevelled down to exhibit the strata.

460.—On a sardonyx. A small modern bust of Hadrian, to the left. Cameo. The topmost layer is of a fine coral red, to which a white stratum succeeds with a gray base.

461.—A cameo in an onyx. A head of Hadrian to the right. A very good modern work cut in a pinkish-white layer on a mottled, reddish base. It is 1½ inch high by 1¾ inch wide. This gem, and No. 452, are in similar settings.

Figured in the " Marlborough Gems," Vol. ii. No. 29.
An Arundel gem, called a Balbinus in the Catalogue (Thec. C, No. 14).

462.—Intaglio on a pale yellow sard. Very fine head of Antoninus Pius to the left. This rare portrait is in the best Roman work of his time.

One of the Chesterfield gems (Cat. No. 45 C).

463.—On a yellowish sard. Intaglio head, probably meant for Antoninus Pius, to the left. Of late and poor Roman work.

An Arundel gem (Cat. Thec. A, No. 20).

464.—Intaglio on a yellowish sard, cracked. A head to the left of Faustina Mater, with her usual head-dress, the hair being wreathed up with pearls. It is a portrait in fair Roman workmanship.

465.—A sapphire ring engraved with the intaglio portrait of Faustina the elder to the left. The work does not look antique, and the likeness is not particularly good. The ring is evidently of oriental, probably Persian, workmanship, the head of the empress having taken the place of an inscription.

An Arundel gem (Cat. Thec. E, No. 15).

466.—A cameo on an amethyst in extremely high relief, representing a full-faced bust of the empress Faustina the elder. She is veiled, perhaps as Proserpine. The work is very fine, and contemporary; it has unfortunately been injured in the nose and cheek.

An Arundel gem (Cat. Thec. C, No. 15).

467.—On a bluish translucent chalcedony. A front-faced cameo bust, in nearly full relief, of Faustina the elder; but in this, as in the last gem, the hair is not dressed in the manner usual in her portraits. She is represented as Juno, her diadem being adorned with real pearls. It is a work of great beauty, and, possibly, antique. Nearly $1\frac{7}{8}$ inch in height.

An Arundel gem (Thec. C, No. 17).

468.—On a singular sardonyx. A cameo portrait in low relief, representing Faustina the elder, to the right. A gem of the renaissance period. The upper layer is pink; the flesh rendered in a blush white, the base being translucent and pink.

From the Arundel Collection (Cat. Thec. B, No. 15).

469.—On a sardonyx. A cameo head of Faustina the elder, to the left. Very beautiful modern work. A bequest to the Duke of Marlborough from the Duchess of Bedford.

470.—On a nicolo. Portrait to the left of Marcus Aurelius. A modern intaglio.

471.—Onyx. Cameo, with conjoined busts of Marcus Aurelius and Faustina. Cinque-cento work, in a white layer on a gray base.

An Arundel gem (Cat. Thec. B, No. 3).

472.—Intaglio on a sard. Portrait of Faustina the younger, to the left. A very rude work of uncertain date.

> From Lord Chesterfield's Collection (Bessb. Cat. No. 20 c).
> Called by Natter Julia Pia Felix.

473.—A cameo on a sardonyx. A small head of Faustina the younger, to the left. Apparently of Roman workmanship. It is cut in a white layer on a dark sard ground.

474.—A sardonyx. A cameo portrait, apparently of Faustina the younger, to the right; ivy-crowned, in a Bacchanal character. The ivy wreath and the rim are reserved in a brown layer. The work is good, and probably of the renaissance period. It is $1\frac{3}{8}$ inch in height by 1 inch.

> An Arundel gem (Cat. Thec. B. No. 10).
> Figured in the "Marlborough Gems," Vol. ii. No. 14, as Libera.

475.—On a sardonyx. A cameo bust attributed to Faustina the younger, to the right. In low relief, exhibiting nevertheless three distinct layers of the stone. Good work, perhaps a portrait of some lady in the 2nd century.

> A Bessborough gem (Cat. No. 8).
> Figured in the "Marlborough Gems," Vol. ii. No. 32, as Lucilla.

476.—On an onyx. A bust portrait of Faustina the younger, to the right. A modern cameo.

> Figured in the "Marlborough Gems," Vol. ii. No. 32, as Lucilla.

477.—Nicolo. A cameo portrait, in low relief, of Lucius Verus, to the left. It is good contemporary work, cut in a bluish-white layer on a black sard base.

> An Arundel gem (Cat. Thec. C, No. 12), termed Ælius Cæsar.

478.—Onyx, opaque white on gray. Renaissance portrait to the right, in cameo, meant probably for Lucius Verus. It is beautifully mounted in a contemporary enamelled setting, with small table diamonds inserted in it.

> A Bessborough gem (Cat. No. 7).

479.—Fine brown sard. A three-quarter bust intaglio, representing Lucilla in the character of Diana. A remarkable gem of good contemporary Roman workmanship.

> One of the Arundel gems (Cat. Thec. A, No. 90).

80 ROMAN AND POST-AUGUSTAN PORTRAITURE.

480.—A magnificent sardonyx 2½ inches high. It is a nicolo-sardonyx; a summit layer of brown is left only on the cornice, the hair and paludamentum; the work is in a bluish-white on a black sard base; the whole bevelled to show the strata. It represents a fine head of Commodus to the right in a cameo. On the reverse is a figure of the IΑΩ Abraxas, rudely worked in intaglio, with the inscription ΑΡΔΟΥ ΓΕΝΝΑΙ ΩΔΕΜΕΝΙ ΒΑϹΙΛΙϹΚΩϹ.

An Arundel gem, termed a Didius Julian (Cat. Thec. D, No. 11).

481.—Cameo on a sardonyx. A three-quarter figure of the young Commodus, to the left. An early renaissance gem. It is 1½ inch high by 1¾ inch wide, and is cut in a white layer on a dark sard base.

From the Arundel Collection (Cat. Thec. C, No. 10).

482.—A cameo on a unique semi-oval sardonyx; of the dimensions of 8¾ inches in width, by 6 inches in height, and therefore ranking among the five most important for their magnitude in existence. It is of all these the most remarkable as a stone, if we consider the quality of its four brilliantly-hued layers, and the parallelism in which they lie superposed. The subject, a pair of imperial heads confronted, is designated as Didius Julian and Manlia Scantilla; these names being engraved on escutcheons on the silver-gilt frame which surrounds the stone, and gives it a rectangular form, while also holding together the four fragments into which this extraordinary sardonyx has at some time been broken. This attribution, however, is very questionable. The difficulty in determining it is increased by the treatment of the subjects. A ram's horn adorns the brow of the emperor, while an oaken (ilex) wreath with acorns surrounds the head. The emblems borne by the empress are not less mixed, for twined with an ilex wreath similar to that of the emperor, are wheat-ears, pomegranates, and poppy heads. A slightly Isiac character is imparted to the empress' attire by a large bow-like knot that ties her fringed robe, similar to the knot ornament (nodus Isiacus) of the priestesses of Isis. A small sphendone-formed tiara furthermore surmounts her forehead. Whether the empress thus personifies Juno or Ceres, or is intended to represent the attributes of both; and whether the emperor unites with the character of the Dodonean Zeus that of Jupiter Ammon or of Bacchus, the style of the work, no less than the character of the heads, would determine the date of the gem to be certainly as late as the Antonine period, when such a multiplicity of attributes was coming into vogue. If the heads represent Didius Julian and his empress—and a resemblance to them is to be recognised, though one much flattered on the side of youthfulness—the cameo could not have been the work of his very short and dearly bought reign. It might, however, have been a work of Byzantine age, wrought, possibly, in the reign of the second Julian, in compliment to his namesake and predecessor; a reign in which the tendencies of the emperor might have tinged the work with what Egyptian colouring its design exhibits. On the other hand, the resemblance of the portraits to those of Marcus Aurelius, or even of Antoninus Pius when young, and Faustina the elder, is considerable; and both in likeness and in the treatment of the imperial paludamentum there is much that recals a large intaglio at St. Petersburg, representing the heads of Marcus Aurelius and Faustina confronted. Indeed, this seems to be much the most probable attribution for these two imperial heads. That they are not portraits of Commodus and Crispina, as Mr. King has suggested, is certain from the fact that Crispina had ceased to be the wife of Commodus before he wore a beard.

The gem itself, as far as the *technique* is concerned, as well from the poverty of the modelling, the absence of character in the features, as from the elaborate treatment of the hair and accessories, might well be a work of the Antonine age, in which these polychrome gems had become the fashion; and we may fairly assume it to have been contemporary with the sovereigns it represents.

On the setting at the back of the gem an inscription is seen running as follows: "Ingens anaglyphicum opus olim Saunesiorum ducum nunc vero pretio acquisitum in Fontesiano cimelio asservatum." A Marquis de Fuentes was an ambassador from Portugal in Rome in the earlier half of the last century, and is mentioned by Raspe and by Mariette as a gem collector. From his collection this great gem may have passed to that of the Duke of Marlborough. But to determine to what ducal family it had previously belonged is more difficult.

The work of the cameo is kept in very flat relief, and the artist has otherwise most ingeniously handled his material, so as to give the most contrasted effects to the various layers of the stone.

Figured in the "Marlborough Gems."

483.—Onyx. A cameo head of Pescennius Niger, to the left. Modern work.

One of the Bessborough gems (Cat. No. 31) called Antoninus.

484.—On a beryl. An intaglio bust of Julia Domna, to the left, in the stiff style of her coins. No doubt a work of the first years of the 3rd century, much re-polished.

One of the Bessborough gems (Cat. No. 20).
Figured in the "Marlborough Gems," Vol. i. No. 24, and also among Worlidge's Etchings.

82 ROMAN AND POST-AUGUSTAN PORTRAITURE.

485.—On a remarkable sapphire, ⅜ inch high, ½ inch wide. An intaglio portrait of Caracalla, to the left; indubitably contemporary, and of good workmanship for his period.

> A gem from the Chesterfield portion of the Bessborough Collection (Cat. No. 8 c). Worlidge has given an etching of it.

486.—On a very fine sard. An intaglio portrait, to the right, apparently of the young Caracalla. The form of the paludamentum indicates it as a work of the late Antonine period, if, indeed, it be not renaissance.

> An Arundel gem (Cat. Thec. A, No. 37).

487.—On a sard. A portrait in intaglio of the young Caracalla, to the left. A work of ordinary merit.

> An Arundel gem (Cat. Thec. A, No. 29), called Elagabalus.

488.—On a sard, prettily set. An intaglio head, to the left, probably of the young Caracalla.

489.—On white Oriental alabaster. A three-quarter face bust, to the right, in very high relief, of Caracalla. The head alone is antique, and measures 1½ inch in length : the bust and ground having been added in modern times. It is a work of much merit for his age.

> From the Bessborough Collection (Cat. No. 25).
> Figured in the "Marlborough Gems," Vol. i. No. 22.

490.—Onyx. A modern portrait in cameo of Caracalla.

491.—Fine pale plasma ; intaglio, three-quarter face. A modern work, possibly representing Geta when young, in the character of Mercury. The caduceus is on his left shoulder.

492.—An onyx cameo portrait, cut in a white layer on a pink gray ground, to the right, of probably Geta when young. The work seems to be of his age.

493.—On a pale citrine, highly foiled. An intaglio profile, to the right, of possibly Elagabalus. He wears a radiate crown and the paludamentum. The style is peculiar, and the gem may

ROMAN AND POST-AUGUSTAN PORTRAITURE. 83

perhaps be a late Roman work, of his time. On the back of the gem a portrait head of a lady is enamelled, on a blue enamel ground.

It was one of the Chesterfield gems (Cat. No. 15 c), termed a Ptolemy. Figured in the "Marlborough Gems," Vol. ii. No. 1, as Ptolemy Auletes. Also among Worlidge's Etchings.

494.—On an onyx, in a whitish-blue layer on a dark bluish-gray ground. A bust, in high relief, of Elagabalus. A rude work, perhaps contemporary.

An Arundel gem (Cat. Thec. B, No. 26).

495.—A sardonyx, 3½ inches high by 2½ inches wide. A fine cameo portrait, to the right, of Julia Paula. This important gem appears to be contemporary work of a very high class for the age of Elagabalus. The face is worked in a white semi-opaque portion of the upper layer, the rest in a transparent layer, while the ground is a mottled sard. The outline seems to have suffered somewhat in point of hardness by a re-polishing of the ground.

An Arundel gem, designated as Julia Domna (Cat. Thec. D, No. 8).

496.—A sardonyx of three layers, 2⅛ inches high by 1¾ inch wide. A cameo profile portrait, to the left, of probably Julia Mammæa, aunt of Elagabalus. The hair and the dress are carefully and strongly rendered in a massive dark brown layer. The face, less carefully finished, is in a white layer, the base layer of the stone being black. It has all the character of a contemporary work.

Probably the Arundel gem designated Antonia (Cat. Thec. D, No. 3)?

497.—A modern cameo portrait to the left. Probably meant for Valerian.

An Arundel gem (Cat. Thec. B, No. 32)?

498.—Forty portrait heads, representing the triumvirs and the emperors down to Valerian. Natter was, without doubt, the engraver, and he states in his Catalogue of the Bessborough gems, that they were copied from coins or antique intaglios, and were wrought on as varied a series of stones as possible.

The order of the Imperial personages is indicated by small

84   ROMAN AND POST-AUGUSTAN PORTRAITURE.

figures cut on the mountings, corresponding to the following attributions :

1. Triumvirate.	21. Lucius Verus.
2. Julius Cæsar.	22. Commodus.
3. Marcus Jun. Brutus.	23. Pertinax.
4. Augustus.	24. Didius Julianus.
5. Tiberius.	25. Pescennius Niger.
6. Caligula.	26. Clodius Albinus.
7. Claudius.	27. Septimius Severus.
8. Nero.	28. Caracalla.
9. Galba.	29. Macrinus.
10. Otho.	30. Elagabalus.
11. Vitellius.	31. Alexander Severus.
12. Vespasian.	32. Maximinus.
13. Titus.	33. Gordian Africanus.
14. Domitian.	34. Balbinus and Pupienus.
15. Nerva.	35. Gordian Pius.
16. Trajan.	36. Philip.
17. Hadrian.	37. Trajan Decius.
18. Ælius.	38. Hostilianus.
19. Antoninus Pius.	39. Æmilianus.
20. Marcus Aurelius.	40. Valerianus.

498A.—A gold stater of Philip II.

498B.—A gold stater of Alexander.

498C.—An oval cameo in silver, representing busts of Augustus and Livia; on the reverse the same subject incased. It is a casting of probably cinque-cento date, mounted in an iron ring, with chased gold shoulders and bezel. This identical ring was figured by Gronovius in Gorlæus' "Dactylotheca" in 1609, No. 183.

   An Arundel gem (Cat. Theo. A, 102).

499.—Sardonyx, 1⅛ inch high by ⅞ths wide. Fine profile portrait to the left, much resembling that attributed to Mæcenas. The head is in an ivory-like upper layer on a yellowish base. The work is very fine and may be of the Augustan age, and is in considerable relief. It is mounted in a very handsome renaissance setting with garnets.

   Figured in the "Marlborough Gems," Vol. ii. No. 22.

500.—A large black sard, 1½ inch high by 1¼ inch wide. An intaglio, representing a head to the left and bust of Antinous, with a spear on his left shoulder. The work is magnificent and worthy of the age of Hadrian. The stone is much shattered,

PORTRAITURE OF UNKNOWN ATTRIBUTION. 85

but not to the destruction of the work. The letters ANTI are all that remain of what was once a legend.

> Figured in the "Marlborough Gems," Vol. i. No. 21, and in Worlidge's Etchings.

500a.—A facsimile of the last, by Burch. Cornelian.

501.—A splendid sard, with an intaglio head, to the left; somewhat like Antinous, with his name so inscribed as to read directly, and with the appearance of antiquity. On the back of the gem are the letters LAI, possibly indicating its owner at a period subsequent to the date of its production.

> Figured in the "Marlborough Gems," Vol. ii. No. 30.
> See Introduction, p. xvii.

501a.—A cameo bust of Antinous to the right, probably of the cinque-cento period.

> An Arundel gem (Cat. Thec. B, No. 4).

502.—Chalcedony. A head of Antinous to the right. Fine work of the last century.

503.—A fine yellow sard. Portrait, to the left, of the Antinous of the bas-relief in the Villa Albani. It is very fine intaglio, and carries the signature of Marchant.

3.—*PORTRAITURE OF UNKNOWN OR UNCERTAIN ATTRIBUTION.*

504.—A cornelian : an intaglio. Head to the left, representing the so-called Genius of the Museum Clementinum. It is a deeply-cut work by Marchant, but not signed by him.

> Purchased for twelve guineas from Marchant.

505.—Intaglio to the right; on a sardonyx. A male head of an unknown personage, excellently finished in a Greek or Greco-Roman style. Natter took it for a Brutus; it has a slight beard.

> A Bessborough gem (Cat. No. 46).

86 PORTRAITURE OF UNKNOWN ATTRIBUTION.

506.—Intaglio on a yellowish sard. Front face male beardless portrait. A work probably contemporary with the person it represents; the treatment of the hair seems to belong to the end of the first century.

> Figured in the "Marlborough Gems," Vol. ii. No. 9.
> A Bessborough gem (Cat. No. 79).

507.—Intaglio on a sard. Male head to the left. Portrait of an unknown personage, apparently of the Augustan period.

> A Bessborough gem, termed by Natter (Cat. No. 81) Cicero.
> Figured under the same name in the "Marlborough Gems," Vol. ii. No. 12, and also among Worlidge's Etchings.

508.—Intaglio on a bluish chalcedony. Portrait to the right. Head of an unknown personage, with the imperial fillet.

> A Bessborough gem, described by Natter (Cat. No. 90) as a head of "Olivier Cromwell, à l'antique."

509.—Intaglio on a pale plum-blue amethyst. A portrait, to the right, of an unknown head; mounted in a beautiful enamelled renaissance setting. The work seems of imperial Roman time.

> It is termed Nerva by Natter (Cat. No. 4 c) in his description of the Bessborough Collection, into which it came from the cabinet of Lord Chesterfield.
> Figured in the "Marlborough Gems," Vol. i. No. 18.

510.—Intaglio on a red jasper. A head, to the left, apparently representing a Barbarian, slightly bearded. It seems to be work of a good imperial age.

> A Chesterfield gem (Cat. No. 12 c), termed by Natter a Tiberius.

511.—Intaglio on a sard; a portrait looking to the left, of an unknown bearded person. The work is vigorous, and probably of the Imperial age.

> A Chesterfield gem (Cat. No. 25 c).

512.—Intaglio on a red paste. A bust portrait to the left, probably made in the last century from an antique original. It may, perhaps, be Geta Cæsar.

PORTRAITURE OF UNKNOWN ATTRIBUTION.   87

513.—Intaglio on a fine sard. A portrait head to the left, which has been attributed to C. Antistius Restio. It has a signature, **CKYΛAKO**, but is a modern work, deeply and finely cut, probably by an Italian hand during the last century.

<small>Figured in the "Marlborough Gems," Vol. ii. 8.</small>

514.—Intaglio on chalcedony. A laureated head to the right, of Roman workmanship.

<small>An Arundel gem, perhaps rightly attributed to Geta in the Catalogue (Ar. Cat. Thec. A, No. 22). The work, however, seems too good for Geta's time.</small>

515.—Intaglio on cornelian. A bust of late Roman period to the right.

516.—Intaglio on a golden sard, to the right. A portrait head, the hair finely worked; of probably early Imperial date.

<small>Termed Marcus Agrippa in the Duke's Catalogue, but it is not like the great Admiral.</small>

517.—Intaglio on a fine sard, to the left. A head, possibly meant for Mæcenas. It is very bald, like the well-known portrait signed "Solon." The stone is broken, and the work seems antique.

<small>An Arundel gem, termed in the Arundel Catalogue (Ar. Cat. Thec. A, 36), a head of Solon.</small>

518.—Intaglio on a pale sard. Two conjugated imperial heads to the left, intended for an emperor and empress. The work is rude, and of the cinque-cento period, and over polished.

<small>An Arundel gem (Ar. Cat. Thec. A, No. 14) called in the Catalogue Augustus and Livia.</small>

519.—Intaglio on a nicolo, to the left. A bearded head with a fillet, rude in workmanship.

520.—Intaglio on a fine yellow sard, to the right. Portrait of a bearded personage, possibly of Clodius Albinus, worked in a remarkable manner, the hair falling in circular wreaths (calamus stratus?). It is a Roman work.

88   PORTRAITURE OF UNKNOWN ATTRIBUTION.

521.—Intaglio on a nicolo, to the left. Portrait head, probably representing some imperial prince in the character of Mercury; the caduceus behind his head, and a tortoise in the field. It is of fair workmanship, but the style and the mode in which the stone is treated give the gem the character of a modern work.

 Figured in the "Marlborough Gems," Vol. i. No. 5, and there denominated M. J. Brutus. It was purchased of a Mr. C. Morison for £60.

522.—Intaglio on a fine red sard, a beardless head, to the left; attributed to Sulla. Finely worked, probably of cinque-cento age.

 One of the Arundel gems (Cat. Thec. A, No. 17).
 Figured in the " Marlborough Gems," Vol. i. No. 2.

523.—Intaglio on cornelian. Portrait bust, to the left, of a youthful personage, probably a son or nephew of one of the early Cæsars, perhaps Germanicus; but the workmanship is rude, and the portrait unrecognisable.

524.—Intaglio on a splendid sard, three-quarter face to the right. A cinque-cento bearded portrait.

 An Arundel gem (Cat. Thec. A, No. 26).

525.—Intaglio in sard. A portrait to the right, with a fillet, of cinque-cento date.

 A Bessborough gem (Cat. No. 76).

526.—Intaglio on a sard to the left. Helmeted bust, modern, or renaissance, in date.

 One of the Chesterfield gems (Cat. No. 17 c), and termed by Natter Philip of Macedon.
 Figured in Worlidge's Etchings.

527.—Intaglio on a sardonyx; a three-quarter faced bust, perhaps meant for Demosthenes. It is a modern work, cut in an upper layer of yellow sard into a white layer, below which is another stratum of yellow sard.

528.—Cameo on an onyx; bust to the left. A minute modern work, the head cut in considerable relief, in a white layer on a bluish-gray ground.

 A Bessborough gem (Cat. No. 94). Natter calls it Democritus.

PORTRAITURE OF UNKNOWN ATTRIBUTION.

529.—Intaglio on a sard. To the left, a finely cut bust portrait, set in a pretty ring.

It was a Medina gem (Bess. Cat. No. 5 M).

530.—Cameo on an onyx. A portrait head to the left, of small size but fine workmanship, dubious as to age; cut in a white layer on a bluish-gray base.

531.—Cameo on a sardonyx. Bust portrait to the right, with a radiate crown of three rays; perhaps some oriental prince, under the Empire, at a late period. The paludamentum and crown are in a brown layer, the face, hair, and neck of a pinkish white supported by a white base layer. He is beardless, and wears an ear-ring.

An Arundel gem (Cat. Thec. B, No. 33).

532.—Cameo on pale blue turquoise, to the left. Portrait of an unknown person, of fine workmanship, and apparently antique.

533.—Cameo, to the right. A bust of a bearded person, cut in a translucent violet-tinted layer of an onyx, with a yellowish base; the hair and the drapery are left in a yellow upper layer.

Attributed by Natter, in the Bessborough Catalogue (No. 33 M), to Marcus Aurelius. It was one of the Medina gems.

534.—A small cameo on an onyx; bust portrait to the right, of renaissance workmanship, representing a warrior in a singular helmet; the helmet and part of the armour left in a white layer.

An Arundel gem (Cat. Thec. A, No. 129).

535.—Cameo, on sardonyx. A portrait of an ecclesiastic to the right. It is a cinque-cento work of a very high character, in somewhat flat relief in a porcelain-white layer on a yellowish brown base.

An Arundel gem (Cat. Thec. B, No. 37).

536.—Cameo on an onyx. A renaissance, three-quarter length, representation of a negro, the drapery being left in a white layer, while the face and arm are represented in a stratum of black.

An Arundel gem (Cat. Thec. A, No. 132).

PORTRAITURE OF UNKNOWN ATTRIBUTION.

537.—Cameo on a fine sardonyx, 2¾ inches high, 1⅝ inch wide. A bust portrait to the left of a helmeted warrior, the ægis and helmet left in a yellowish-brown layer, face in a whitish layer on a dark gray ground. It is a fine work of the cinque-cento period.

538.—Cameo on an onyx, to the right. A very celebrated head, cut by Alessandro Cesari (Il Greco). It is not bearded, yet it has been called the portrait of Phocion; probably from a supposed similarity to the known gem with the inscription ΦΩΚΙΩΝΟC. That gem was pronounced by Vasari, in his life of A. Cesari, to be the *ne plus ultra* of the engraver's art. This cameo is 1¾ inch high, by 1½ inch wide, the face being cut in an opaque white layer in rather shallow relief, on a reddish-brown base. It is splendidly mounted in an enamelled setting, forming a rich wreath of flowers, among which a sunflower recurs conspicuously. It is evidently a replica.

Figured in the "Marlborough Gems," Vol. i. No. 28.
This gem, with the Horatius Cocles, No. 596, the Antinous, No. 501, and Matidia, probably the Sabina, No. 455, was bought by the third Duke for 600*l.* from Zanetti. See Introduction, p. xvii.

539.—Cameo on sardonyx. Small imperial bust to the right, in a whitish-blue layer on a dark gray ground, the hair and a raised border showing a layer of yellow. The work does not seem ancient.

An Arundel gem (Cat. Thec. A, No. 113), called an Antinous.

540.—Cameo on onyx; a negro's head, full face. Renaissance work, in a dark upper layer on a white ground.

An Arundel gem (Cat. Thec. A, 126).

541.—Cameo on onyx; a heroic head to the left. A very fine modern work, cut out of a flesh-coloured layer with a black base.

Figured as Caracalla in the "Marlborough Gems," Vol. i. No. 23.

542.—Cameo on onyx. Head, to the right, of an old man, wrinkled and bald. It may be an ancient work, but it is of very dubious age. It is in its favour that it was an Arundel gem (Cat. Thec. B, No. 5), where it is attributed to Caius Antius Restio, whose portrait occurs on consular coins when his son was a moneyer.

PORTRAITURE OF UNKNOWN ATTRIBUTION.

543.—Cameo on a cat's eye. A head of an unknown person to the left.

   A Bessborough gem (Cat. No. 91).

544.—Cameo on an onyx. A modern portrait, to the left, cut in a white layer on a transparent ground.

   A Bessborough gem (Cat. No. 18).
   Figured in the "Marlborough Gems," Vol. i. No. 1, as Scipio Africanus.

545.—Intaglio on a red jasper. Two heads, viz. those of a Roman lady and her child, apparently of the Antonine period.

   An Arundel gem, called in the Catalogue (Thec. A, No. 16) Agrippina and Drusus.

546.—Intaglio on brown sard. Two Roman (male and female) bust portraits, confronted; probably of private individuals of the age of Caracalla, the head-dress of the lady resembling that of Plautilla.

   Probably an Arundel gem (in the Cat. Thec. A, No. 27).

547.—Intaglio on a sard. Bust portraits, male and female, in rude workmanship of the late Middle Empire. They may be intended to represent Carinus and Magnia Urbica.

   An Arundel gem, called in the Catalogue (Thec. A, No. 21) portraits of Antoninus Pius and Faustina.

548.—Intaglio on a burnt sard. Female head to the left; the hair in particular is burnt in. It seems to be Roman work.

   An Arundel gem, termed Faustina (Cat. Thec. B, No. 28).

549.—Intaglio on amethyst; portrait of a lady to the left. A work probably of the second century.

   An Arundel gem (Cat. Thec. A, No. 24), called Crispina.

550.—Intaglio head on a red jasper to the left, of a lady with head-dress similar to one of those among the Cyrene marbles at the British Museum. Probably of the Antonine period.

PORTRAITURE OF UNKNOWN ATTRIBUTION.

551.—Intaglio on a ruby sard. Portrait to the left, apparently of a Roman lady, mounted in a ring of extraordinary beauty, full-length figures forming either shank, while on the back of the bezel there are little birds.

One of the Chesterfield gems in the Bessborough Collection (Cat. No. 9 c), called Lucilla, and so figured in Worlidge's Etchings. Natter terms the stone a "Berill rouge."

552.—Intaglio on a fine sard. Bust to the left, apparently of a lady, but with a caduceus on the shoulder, whence it has been supposed to represent an imperial youth, but the portrait is not that of any young Cæsar. It seems to be Roman work of about the Antonine period.

553.—Intaglio on a sard. A modern female head to the left.

A Bessborough gem (Cat. No. 26 c).

554.—Intaglio on a nicolo, with brown base-layer. Renaissance female head to the left.

From the Arundel Collection (Cat. Thec. A, No. 77).

555.—Intaglio on a nicolo. Modern portrait to the left.

556.—A small modern cameo on an onyx, cut in a red layer on a translucent white base, under which lies a blue stratum. It represents a female head to the left.

557.—Cameo on a splendid sardonyx of $1\frac{5}{8}$ inch in length, by $1\frac{1}{2}$ inch in width. Portrait to the left, veiled, with a sceptre, probably of an empress, but it is impossible to identify it. It may represent Julia Mæsa, and certainly does not seem earlier than the time of Elagabalus. The face and a reserved rim are in white, the hair and the veil are in a rich brown layer, the robe in one of a paler hue of brown.

One of the Arundel gems (Cat. Thec. D, No. 1), called Julia Mæsa.

559.—Cameo on sardonyx. Female head to the right; the face in a white opaque layer. The abundant and boldly worked hair left in a yellow tint, the base being black. It is a beautiful but renaissance work, though worthy of the hand of a Greek artist.

PORTRAITURE OF UNKNOWN ATTRIBUTION.

560.—Cameo on onyx. Small female head to the right; cut in a porcelain-white layer on a dark gray ground. It is antique in character.

561.—Cameo on sardonyx. Portrait to the right; bust of a lady in a head-dress of the fashion of the time of Titus. The reserved rim and head are cut in a brown layer on a white ground. It is shallow work, well finished, and probably cinque-cento in date.

An Arundel gem (Cat. Thec. B, No. 8).

562.—Cameo on a sard. Portrait of a lady to the right, in a dress of the early sixteenth century; the face being apparently artificially whitened, or possibly cut on a white mark in the stone. It is a renaissance work in high relief.

An Arundel gem (Cat. Thec. B, No. 16), called Sappho.

563.—Cameo on onyx. Bust portrait of a lady to the right. Renaissance work, cut in a white stratum on a gray base.

Perhaps an Arundel gem called a Livia (Cat. Thec. B, No. 14).

564.—Cameo on an onyx. Veiled bust portrait to the right of a lady, cut in a white stratum on one of pinkish gray. A renaissance work.

An Arundel gem (Ar. Cat. Thec. D, No. 6).

565.—Cameo on a sardonyx. Portrait to the left of a lady, cut in a white layer, with a base of dark sard. Perhaps contemporary, in work as in subject, with the beautiful setting, which is formed of a hollow wreath of flowers exquisitely enamelled in colours, the back being adorned with deep blue enamel and black arabesque work, which is much in the style of Laudin, who worked about the middle of the seventeenth century.

566.—Cameo on a magnificent onyx, 3 inches by $1\frac{7}{8}$ inch. A lady in a veil, represented by a bust portrait to the left; the design, in an oval form, being supported by an acanthus flower. It is very beautiful work, the figure and a reserved rim cut in flat relief out of a rich dark brown layer with a base of white. It is by some admirable cinque-cento artist.

An Arundel gem (Cat. Thec. D, No. 4).

567.—Cameo on a sardonyx; bust to the right of a lady. A pretty cinque-cento work, in a white upper layer of the stone, with a transparent yellow base layer.

An Arundel gem (Cat. Thec. A, No. 130).

568.—Cameo on an onyx. A head to the right. Modern portrait of a lady, but much mutilated.

569.—Cameo on an onyx. Portrait to the left, much undercut; it is a good work of the cinque-cento period.

570.—Cameo on onyx. Two conjugated and helmeted female heads to the right; perhaps representing deities. The helmets of each are left in a pale red stratum, the faces and ground being white. The gem has all the appearance of an antique.

571.—Cameo on jasper onyx. Three-quarter face and bust of a negress; an asp inflicting a wound on her bosom. It is a renaissance work, cut in a layer of black jasper, on a sard base. The stone is bevelled off all round, and is of the dimensions of $2\frac{1}{4}$ inches in height, and $1\frac{3}{4}$ inch in width.

A Bessborough gem, termed Cleopatra, for whom, doubtless, the renaissance artist intended the African features (Cat. No. 16).

572.—A cameo on an onyx; being a head and bust to the left, in a white layer on a base of an amethyst tint.

An Arundel gem (Ar. Cat. Thec. B, No. 9), called a head of Berenice.

573.—Cameo on onyx. A modern female head to the right, cut in a white layer on a black ground.

One of the Bessborough gems (Cat. No. 77).

574.—Cameo on chalcedony. A modern much undercut portrait of a lady to the right.

575.—Cameo on an onyx. Head of a lady to the right in a white layer, on bluish gray. Modern or renaissance work. On the back is an intaglio: figures of a lady and a boy.

Probably an Arundel gem (Cat. Thec. B, No. 13).

PORTRAITURE OF UNKNOWN ATTRIBUTION.

576.—Cameo on a pretty sardonyx, with a female head to the left, wearing a sort of mural crown. A bevelled rim left round the head, exhibiting a yellow layer beside the brownish layer in which the head is cut, in flat relief with a white ground: either a modern or a renaissance gem.

Perhaps an Arundel gem (Cat. Thec. B, No. 28).

577.—Cameo on onyx. A female head, of poor modern workmanship.

578.—Cameo in very flat relief on a sardonyx of the finest quality; $2\frac{1}{2}$ inches in length, by $1\frac{5}{8}$ inch in width. It is a bust portrait to the right, in a bluish layer on a black ground, traces of a brown surface layer being left in the hair and robe. It is probably renaissance work.

An Arundel gem (Cat. Thec. D, No. 10), termed Junia Claudia.

579.—Cameo on sardonyx, $2\frac{1}{4}$ inches in length, by $1\frac{1}{2}$ inch in breadth. A modern or perhaps a renaissance work. Portrait of a lady, in one-third length figure, turning her back, face looking to the right, in a white translucent layer on a dark ground. It is mounted in a rococo setting of the time of Louis XV. (?), carrying enamelled trophies, and ten small sardonyxes and onyxes.

Possibly an Arundel gem, termed Cleopatra (Ar. Cat. Thec. D, No. 5).

580.—A large cameo on an onyx, with two different layers of pinkish white; 2 inches by 1 inch in dimensions, representing a female head in the most florid style of the renaissance.

Perhaps an Arundel gem, termed Octavia (Ar. Cat. Thec. B, No. 6).

581.—Cameo on onyx. A negress head in front face. A renaissance work, cut in a brown layer on a bluish-white base.

582.—Intaglio on a chalcedony. Head to the right, by Marchant; a beautiful and elaborate work, recorded in the handwriting of the third Duke of Marlborough as being a copy from a work by Fiamingo; a head of Susannah.

4.—*PORTRAITURE OF MODERN PERSONAGES.*

583.—Intaglio on a spinel-ruby. A deeply cut minute head in front face, wearing a coronet with fleurs-de-lis. It is set in a contemporary gold ring, with the words "Tel il nest"—"There is none such as he," inscribed on the ring.
This most interesting and minute intaglio is in all probability the identical signet of Charles V. of France, described in the inventory of his valuables, made in 1379 : " Le signet du Roy qui est de la teste d'un roy sans barbe ; et est d'un fin rubis d'Orient : c'est celui de quoi le roy scelle les lettres qu'il escript de sa main." It accords exactly with the head surmounting the royal figure on his coins ; and it is a most interesting gem, as illustrating the skill of the gem engraver at so early an age as the fourteenth century.

    An Arundel gem (Cat. Thec. A, No. 27), termed in the Catalogue a Lombard king.

584.—Cameo on a sardonyx. A minute portrait to the right, probably meant for Charles V., cut in a shallow manner in a white layer on a dark gray ground, with traces of an upper yellow layer on the hair and collar.

    An Arundel gem (Cat. Thec. A, No. 128).

585.—Cameo on an onyx. Portrait to the left. The hair in a yellowish layer, face in one of whitish blue, on ground of bluish gray. It is early renaissance work, representing apparently some personage of that period, perhaps Cosmo de Medici ; called, however, in the Arundel Catalogue (Thec. A, No. 104), Clodius Albinus.

586.—Cameo on a fine sardonyx. Portrait to the right of Philip II., apparently by Jacopo da Trezzo. It is beautifully cut in a clear white layer, with a base of sard ; at the back there is an eagle standing on a serpent, a mountainous country behind, a motto engraved round it, " Nihil est quod non tolleret qui perfectè diligit."

    A gem from the Bessborough Collection (Cat. No. 12).

587.—Cameo on crystal. Portrait of Philip II. to the left. It is cut in rather low relief by an admirable hand; it carries on the collar ·A·E·, perhaps the signature of the artist.

>An Arundel gem (Cat. Thec. B, No. 35).

588.—A small cameo on a sapphire, representing Henri IV. of France; without doubt a contemporary work.

>A Bessborough gem, termed Gustavus Adolphus (Cat. No. 89).

589.—Cameo on onyx. A contemporary portrait to the left of Mary Queen of Scots. It is in rather high relief, and is mounted in the original blue enamel gold locket, with fleurs-de-lis: it is cut in a white layer with a gray base.

590.—Cameo on sardonyx. Portrait, with bust, to the right, of Cardinal Mazarin; boldly cut, though in low relief, in a yellow layer on a light mottled ground. Contemporary work.

>A Bessborough gem (Cat. No. 11).

591.—Cameo on a sard. A bust portrait, to the left, in very flat relief, probably representing Diana of Poitiers, carrying a quiver behind her. The reverse is a Venus and Cupid. See No. 132.

>An Arundel gem (Cat. Thec. B, No. 22).

592.—Cameo on a sardonyx. A portrait to the right, in rather high relief and fine execution, of a lady, supposed by Mr. Way to be Lady Alathea Talbot, wife of Lord Arundel. It is surrounded by a setting of enamelled gold, with ten garnets engraved with clasped hands; having been probably a wedding gift. The hair and the drapery are worked in two different shades of red, the face in a white layer, while the ground is black. A third red layer, elsewhere cut away, is employed for the left shoulder. On the back is enamelled a gold tressure on a blue ground.

>It was an Arundel gem (Cat. Thec. C, No. 8), and as the above attribution is not assigned to it in the Catalogue, its correctness is improbable.

593.—An intaglio on yellow quartz. Small contemporary portrait to the right of James II.

>A Bessborough gem (Cat. No. 84).

III.—SUBJECTS FROM HISTORY AND DAILY LIFE, Etc.

1.—*HISTORICAL SUBJECTS.*

594.—Intaglio on a large striped agate. The allocution of Pescennius Niger; who is represented addressing the Syrian Legions, and in the act of landing. It is a cinque-cento work, set so as to be worn as a medallion; an octahedron of spinel adorns the ring for suspension.

An Arundel gem (Cat. Thec. E, No. 19).

595.—Cameo on an onyx, representing Horatius Cocles defending the bridge. A marvel of cinque-cento work, on account of the multitude of figures, and the minuteness with which they are delineated. Mars is represented appearing in clouds, and together with the bridge and exaggerated figures upon it, he is rendered in a white layer, on a base of gray.

An Arundel gem (Cat. Thec. B, No. 42).

596.—Cameo on an onyx. Same subject as the last, but finished still more minutely. The hero is represented on horseback, and he and the other figures are not less heroic in proportions than in No. 595. It is probably a work of the 17th century.

See Introduction, p. xvii.

2.—*DIVINATION, SACRIFICES, &c.*

597.—Intaglio on a large sard, an inch in length. A full-length figure seated, and holding downwards a twig or wand, perhaps an augur taking the auspices. The anatomy is not good enough for an antique artist.

DIVINATION—SACRIFICES, &c.

598.—Intaglio on a pale garnet. A priestess going to a sacrifice raising an incense vessel before her: a lighted torch in the field perhaps indicates, as Mr. King has suggested, the nocturnal character of the Dionysian rites. Very fine Roman work.

An Arundel gem (Cat. Thec. A, No. 78).

599.—Cameo on lapis lazuli. Veiled female bust to the left, somewhat like the Philistis on the coins of Syracuse, called by Natter a Sibyl. Probably modern work.

From the Bessborough Collection (Cat. No. 29).

600.—Intaglio on a pale plasma. A representation of a sacrifice; a man carrying the implements of sacrifice on his head, drags a goat towards a little altar, on which a woman drops incense, behind her a Satyr plays the double pipes. It exhibits the elegant drawing but rude *technique* characteristic of the work on this stone, which was so much in use after the middle of the first century.

601.—Intaglio on a hyacinthine garnet. A simple female figure carrying a plate of fruit in her left hand, and a small cantharus in her right, proceeds to a sacrifice. An elegant modern work, by one of the masters of the last century.

602.—A small cameo on sardonyx, representing a sacrifice to Jupiter, offered apparently by a bearded Bacchus, and Pan, Apollo, and two female personages. A well engraved and curious little work of the cinque-cento time, in a white layer on a translucent red base.

It was one of the Medina gems (Bess. Cat. No. 35 M).

603.—Cameo on sardonyx. A woman going to a nocturnal sacrifice; a little girl precedes her carrying a flambeau in one hand and an œnochoë in the other. It is cut in a white ivory layer on a base of brown. The work, particularly the drapery, is excellent, and belongs to an early period of Imperial Rome.

An Arundel gem (Cat. Thec. B, No. 46).
Figured in the "Marlborough Gems," Vol. i. No. 43.

3.—WAR.

604.—Intaglio on a cornelian. The arms of a warrior, including the sword, greaves, and helmet hung on a date palm; a ram, representing perhaps Aries as a horoscope, is under the tree; over it the letters MEANDER, Meander, or perhaps Menander, in ligature: doubtless the name of the owner. The drawing is rude, and yet the work is delicate, and probably of an early Imperial date. Mr. King suggests that this gem may refer to the defeat by Lucullus of Menander, the general of Mithridates. It would seem with more probability to represent the dedication by a Gladiator of his arms and accoutrements after an agonistic victory.

One of the Bessborough gems (Cat. No. 68).

605.—Intaglio on a nicolo. A combat between a warrior and an amazon. Late Roman work.

One of the Chesterfield gems (Bessb. Cat. No. 33 c).

606.—Intaglio on a yellow sard. A Thessalian horseman, distinguished by his hat. The horse has the sash of victory (tenia) depending from his head. The drawing is spirited, though the work is rude; it is probably by a late Greek artist. The figure recals one on coins of Larissa and on those of Alexander of Pheræ.

607.—Intaglio on a pale green plasma. A fallen archer is extracting a spear from his side, while he holds in his right hand a bow. Another warrior is defending him with spear and shield. The work is in fine shallow engraving in the Greek style; but the form of the shield is Roman, and the work belongs, probably, to the early Imperial times, when the plasma was beginning to come into vogue.

Figured in the "Marlborough Gems," Vol. i. No. 42.

608.—Intaglio on a sard, about $1\frac{1}{2}$ inch in height, by $\frac{5}{8}$ths of an inch in width. A warrior, nude, with his shield and armour by his side, stands in front of a horse, whose bridle he holds, but which is very rudely drawn. Probably Greek work of not very early date.

It was in the Arundel Collection (Ar. Cat. Thec. E, No. 16).
Figured as Alexander and Bucephalus in the "Marlborough Gems," Vol. i. No. 45.

609.—Intaglio on a sard. Three warriors (the Horatii) in three-quarter length busts, full-faced; one of them carries a shield with a gryphon killing a deer for a cognisance: the central figure has upon his breast-plate a head, perhaps of Medusa. It is good Roman work, deeply sunk, but of not very early Imperial date.

<small>Figured in the "Marlborough Gems," Vol. i. No. 41.
Purchased by the third Duke for thirty guineas; see Introduction, p. xvii.</small>

610.—Intaglio on a sard. A warrior on horseback, guided by Pallas. A late Roman work of extreme rudeness.

611.—Intaglio on a nicolo. A galley very rudely cut. Both the subject and the treatment are late Roman in character.

612.—Intaglio on a fine sardonyx, with a thick upper layer of sard, and an under layer of transparent bluish chalcedony. It represents a full-length nude figure, with the left arm extended, and the right drawn back to the ear, as if in the act of pulling an arrow, or perhaps a boxer about to deliver a blow: in the latter case it may represent Pollux. The head is somewhat after the type of Hercules. The gem has been entirely re-polished, and is set in a beautiful enamelled mounting, with a white ground and coloured flowers. The work is fine, but it is difficult to assign a date to it, though the anatomy is hardly good enough for an antique artist.

<small>An Arundel gem (Cat. Theo. E, No. 6).</small>

613.—Intaglio on a fine sardonyx, with a rich brown upper layer on a white base, and a narrow intermediate yellowish layer. The same singular subject as the last, but the workmanship is inferior.

614.—Intaglio on a large convex sardonyx, with a deep brown upper layer passing into a white under layer, representing a Greek horseman, with lance and circular buckler, riding at full speed. The work may be Greek, but the drawing is not of much refinement; or it may be a Roman gem of the Consular period, when this form occurs on coins.

615.—A large cameo on onyx, cut in an opaque white layer, and representing a warrior in bust to the left, with helmet and armour most elaborately ornamented. It is undercut, and in very high relief, and a work of the renaissance.

<small>This gem came into the Bessborough Cabinet from the Medina Collection. It had before been in that of Lord Halifax. It passed for King Pyrrhus (Bessb. Cat. No. 38 M).
Figured in the "Marlborough Gems," Vol. ii. No. 7.</small>

616.—Cameo on a small onyx, representing a cavalry combat ; one standard having the letters S·P·Q·R. An elaborate little gem of the cinque-cento time.

617.—An intaglio on a large yellow paste. A Roman warrior riding down a foe. It is a subject frequent as a reverse on Imperial Roman coins, from Trajan to Probus, or even to Constantine. This paste must have been taken from a noble gem.

From the Molinari Cabinet.

618.—Intaglio on a thin yellow sard, with a white rim reserved round it, or afterwards cemented on. It is a little microscopic subject of a warrior and a female shaking hands. It is scratched in with the point, and carries the signature L. S. of Louis Siries, a French engraver of the last century.

619.—Intaglio on a fine banded agate. Four figures ; a man who is seated receives a person, behind whom stand two warriors. Possibly a gem recorded by the Duke of Marlborough as "four figures by Natter." The work is in every way worthy of his master hand.

620.—Intaglio on a yellow paste. A triumphal procession. A wretched modern work, with the pretentious inscription, **ΤΡΥΦΩΝ ΕΠΟΙΕ**.

620 *a*.—Cameo on onyx ; a minute gem, on which a bearded warrior stands between two female personages. On one hand is a trophy, on the other a youth sacrifices at an altar. It is probably a late Roman work, referring to a victory.

An Arundel gem (Cat. Thec. A, No. 134).

620 *b*.—Fragment of a large cameo on sardonyx. On the ground is a prostrate barbarian female figure, in an attitude of grief ; another figure seems as though blowing a trumpet, while a horse bears a large German shield. The work is extremely fine, perhaps part of a subject representing the triumph of Drusus. The mourning figure, the herald and the horse are rendered in a fine white layer, the rest in a pale brownish sard layer.

This was an Arundel gem (Ar. Cat. B, No. 47).
Figured in the "Marlborough Gems," Vol. i. No. 47.

4.—THE GAMES. THE THEATRE.

621.—Intaglio on a fine hyacinthine paste. An athlete with the lettering **∵ ∷ ∴ : OY**, which may be read either as **ΓΝΑΙΟΥ** or **ΓΗΑΙΟΥ**: but the letters have been polished away till only the points remain. In the field is a tripod with a jar. It has been described as an athlete anointing himself. It may, however, be a representation of the subject of the Diadumenos of Polycletus, of which the statue in the British Museum is supposed to be a copy, and which represents an athlete binding a diadem round his head. The gem has been ruinously repolished to show the beauty of a material always hitherto taken for a stone worthy of so fine a work. It may have been wrought by an artist of the Græco-Roman school; and it is deeply and delicately engraved on the flat surface of the glass, which is worked by the tool exactly as if it had been a veritable sard. Natter seems to have taken this material, which he terms in his treatise a "vermilion," for a variety of garnet, and justly considers the flatness of its face exceptional. In his Catalogue, however, he calls it "un Berill d'une beauté achevée" (see No. 43).

It was from the Bessborough Collection (Cat. No. 36), and was formerly the property of Clement V., and afterwards successively in the cabinets of the Apostolo Zeno and of Stosch.

Figured in the "Marlborough Gems," Vol. i. No. 35, where the stone is described as a hyacinthine Sardine approaching the Hyacinth, called by the Italians Giacinto Guarnacino.

621a.—Intaglio on a yellowish sard. A copy of the last, possibly by Natter's inimitable hand, even the polished down character of the surface and the lettering of the name being precisely copied. This gem is an admirable illustration of the way in which antique gems could be copied in the last century.

621b.—A cameo by Marchant, in white on black, on an onyx; also an admirable copy from the famous gem described in 621.

622.—Intaglio on a very fine ruby sard, nearly circular in form. A Discobolus with all the appearance of being good Greek work. The circular form of the gem may be itself in allusion to that of the disc.

One of the Medina gems (Bessb. Cat. No. 2 M).
Figured among Worlidge's Etchings.

623.—Intaglio on an oblong sard, slightly convex. A Discobolus, somewhat lengthy in the drawing; a not very early Roman work of Imperial time. Set in a finely enamelled seal, adorned with fleurs-de-lis.

624.—Intaglio on a red sard with a " chevron "-formed streak across it. A horse stands with a youth by him who reins him in. It is enclosed in the "Etruscan" border, and is rendered in the shallow manner and with the delicate *technique* of the early Greek style, while also the rein of the horse carries the bosses characteristic of the Greek bridle.

One of the Arundel gems (Cat. Thec. A, No. 63).
Figured among the Etchings of Worlidge.

625.—Intaglio on a cornelian. A small quadriga of Roman workmanship.

A Bessborough gem (Cat. No. 45).

626.—Intaglio on a banded agate. An actor in front of a mask on a Term, studying his part. It is Greco-Roman work.

A Bessborough gem (Cat. No. 62).

627.—Intaglio on a very fine oblong convex sard. A figure, apparently, of a comic actor carrying the hooked cane, his attribute. It is spiritedly drawn, and rather deeply cut ; probably rather late Greek work. A gem in the Payne Knight Collection, British Museum, represents a similar subject.

From the Medina Collection (Bessb. Cat. No. 9 M).

5.—DOMESTIC AND PASTORAL OCCUPATIONS.

628.—A poor intaglio copy on cornelian of the famous signet of Michael Angelo, by Gio. Maria da Pescia, in the Bibliothèque Impériale at Paris.

629.—Intaglio on a sard. A sculptor chiselling a bust : a star in the field, and also a Term with a palm branch (of modern introduction ? to conceal part of the Term), a wreath, and a vase. Perhaps a prize to a successful competitor. Greek or

Greco-Roman work. At the back is the symbolic word **IXΘYC** directly written.

A Bessborough gem (Cat. No. 51).

630.—Intaglio on a little nicolo, representing two persons, perhaps children, rolling two large discs along the ground like the modern Italian ruzzuoli. It is good Roman work.

631.—Intaglio on a fine nicolo. A poulterer carrying on a pole over his shoulders a rabbit and a cock. A nice Roman gem.

632.—Intaglio on a very fine nicolo. Huntsman accompanied by a dog, carrying a rabbit on a pole. Very rude late Roman work.

633.—Intaglio on a nicolo. Herdsman driving a cow. Roman work.

One of the Medina gems, termed by Natter Argus watching Io (Bessb. Cat. No. 8 M).

634.—Intaglio on a nicolo. A herdsman yoking a bull, having put a ladder against the animal in order to raise the yoke. Rude Roman work.

635.—Cameo, or *intaglio rilevato*; a very large oval bloodstone, on which a girl is represented in the manner of Egyptian cameo or carvesque work, as though balancing the astragalus. It seems a modern work, apparently copied from a bas-relief.

636.—Cameo on an onyx. A work of the late renaissance period, in which a male and female figure are represented; the former seated, the latter apparently coming to him for protection. The figures and reserved rim are worked in a brown layer.

An Arundel gem (Cat. Thec. C, No. 20).

637.—Intaglio on a sard. A Spinthriate subject.

One of the Medina gems (Cat. No. 11 M).

6.—*URNS, SOUVENIRS, &c.*

638.—Intaglio on a sard. An urn with a basket-work pattern, and two handles formed as of the head and neck of a bird. Roman work.

An Arundel gem (Cat. Thec. A, No. 72).

639.—Intaglio on a fine nicolo. A vase; by Marchant.

640.—Intaglio on a sard. Female head to the left, in a head-dress of the latter part of the second century; rudely worked, with the direct inscription ΕΥΠΟΡΙ ΑΙΑ ΠШΤΙΑ, "May you ever prosper, Potia." The spelling, like the work, almost barbarous; probably a portrait presented to the lady on some auspicious occasion.

641.—Intaglio on a bloodstone. A hand holding out a dead mouse. Fair work of the second century.

642.—Cameo on an onyx; with the device of a hand pinching an ear, and the direct circumscription ΜΝΗΜΟΝΕΥΕ. The device is left in a white layer on a black ground. It is a late Roman work.

One of the Medina gems (Cat. No. 18 M).

643.—Cameo on an onyx. A hand twitching an ear, "aurem vellit," with the direct superscription ΜΝΗΜΟΝΕΥΕ ΜΟΥ ΤΗC ΚΑΛΗC ΨΥΧΗC ΕΥΤΥΧΙ CШΦΡΟΝΙ. "Remember me, your pretty love, good luck to you, Sophronios:" being a souvenir from a lady. Between the device and the lettering there runs a curious thong, as if articulated, with four knots; perhaps as Mr. King suggests, the "Heracleus nodus," symbol of wedlock. The gem is cut in extremely flat relief and much worn, but recals in its manner the early Byzantine work. It is probably of the fourth century. The device is cut in a thin greenish layer, supported by a horny understratum.

644.—Cameo with an inscription, cut directly in a thin white layer of an onyx, with a black base. ΕΥΤΥΧΙ ΒΕΡΟΝΙΚΗ. "May you prosper, O Berenice" (or Veronica). Late Roman work.

IV.—CHRISTIAN AND MEDIÆVAL SUBJECTS.

645.—Intaglio on a fine Bohemian garnet cut *en cabochon*, representing St. Michael and Lucifer. It is a fine work of the renaissance period.

One of the Arundel gems (Cat. Thec. C, No. 23).

646.—Cameo on an onyx. The Madonna of the Assumption standing on the head of a winged angel, four similar angels' heads being arranged on each side of her; the Madonna's hands are clasped. Cut in a white layer in rather high relief on a bluish base. It is a poor work of the renaissance, but mounted in a rich gold setting of a vine stem carrying vine leaves.

One of the Arundel gems (Cat. Thec. C, No. 24).

647.—A minute cameo. A head cut in a white layer on a red base. An early renaissance work, described by Natter as John the Baptist.

From the Bessborough Collection (Cat. No. 88).

648.—Three figures of saints, worked on a sard, the forms being left in the original colour of the stone, the rest being wrought in white by the action of an alkali on the surface. The figures have tints imparted to them by colours painted under the translucent stone. It was a fanciful mode of working in the sixteenth century.

649.—A representation, by a similar treatment of the surface of a red sard, of the entry of Christ into Jerusalem. It is a good composition with many figures.

650.—A shell cameo, slightly convex, representing the Three Kings (of Cologne); cut in pink layers of a shell. It is fair work of cinque-cento time. One of the heads is represented in darker layers than the rest, as representing Africa, and contrasted with the others representing Europe and Asia.

A Bessborough gem (Cat. No. 79).

V.—MASKS, CAPRICES, AND ANIMAL FORMS.

1.—*MASKS.*

651.—Intaglio on a cornelian. Three-quarter face comic mask, with the name KVINTIL. The name seems genuine, and probably recalls the Roman owner of the gem.

    A Bessborough gem (Cat. No. 39).

652.—Intaglio on a bright red jasper. Tragic and comic masks conjoined. A late but fine Roman work.

    A Bessborough gem (Cat. No. 41).

653.—Intaglio on a most excellent nicolo. A comic bearded mask of fine and rather early workmanship.

    A Bessborough gem (Cat. No. 63).

654.—Intaglio on a good nicolo. A Satyric mask with the lettering ΛΟΥΚΤΕΙ. The lettering is certainly genuine, but is difficult of interpretation. It is a fine antique work, and was formerly in the Collection of Gorlæus : vide Dactyl. No. 506.

    A Bessborough gem (Cat. No. 65).

655.—Intaglio on a sard. A full-faced mask of a Davus or comic slave (the Buffoon). An excellent early Imperial work.

    A Bessborough gem (Cat. No. 64).

656.—Intaglio on a sard. A Silenus mask in front face. Very fine work of early Imperial days.

    One of the Chesterfield gems, termed by Natter a bust of Plato (Cat. No. 22 c).

MASKS.

657.—Intaglio on a mottled chalcedony. Small comic mask, perhaps representing the "old man" (the *iratus Chremes*, as Mr. King suggests). Spirited early Roman work.

One of the Medina gems (Cat. No. 6 M, termed a Nicolo).

658.—Intaglio on a nicolo. A small comic mask. Fair Roman work.

A Medina gem (Cat. No. 26 M).

659.—Intaglio on a nicolo. A comic mask, of the time of the third century.

660.—Intaglio on a sard. Two masks, representing Socrates and Xantippe confronted. A very clever and minute work of the best Roman period.

A Medina gem (Bess. Cat. No. 17 M).

661.—Intaglio on a sard. Two masks conjoined; a late Roman work.

A Medina gem (Cat. No. 15 M).

662.—Intaglio on a splendid blood sard. A beautiful caprice, representing a female head conjoined with two Silenus masks. Extremely fine Roman work.

One of the Arundel gems (Cat. Thec. A, No. 6).

663.—Intaglio on golden sard. A very beautiful mask of the Bearded Bacchus. Fine and somewhat early Greek workmanship.

An Arundel gem (Cat. Thec. A, No. 65).

664.—Intaglio on a fine sard. Three masks, resembling heads of Hercules, Apollo, and Bacchus, with the pedum beneath them. Fine early Roman work, set in a beautiful ring.

An Arundel gem (Cat. Thec. A, No. 4).

665.—Intaglio on a red sard. A deeply cut mask of a Cyclops, highly vigorous in its expression. Probably Roman work of the best Imperial time.

Figured among Worlidge's Etchings.

MASKS.

666.—Intaglio on a poor jasper. A mask and a wild boar's head conjugated opposite ways. Under them are written the letters ΘΙΕ, perhaps a play on a word of which the design forms part.

667.—Intaglio on a minute *cabochon* garnet. An "aged" mask; good work for a stone which rarely has fine work upon it.

668.—Intaglio on a banded agate cut *en cabochon*. It is a tragic mask of fine Roman workmanship.

669.—Intaglio on a yellow sard. A mask like a clown's head, with the mouth formed of a scallop shell: probably representing a fountain.

670.—Cameo on a splendid blood-red sard. A fine mask, nearly full-face; probably antique.

671.—Intaglio on a banded agate, with a group of four masks and the name **HELENA** across the gem. It is probably a modern work.

A Bessborough gem (Cat. No. 3 c).

672.—Intaglio on a mottled green and yellow jasper. Three conjoined masks: a modern work.

One of the Chesterfield gems (Cat. No. 44 c).

673.—Cameo on a sard. A Satyric mask in high relief, probably of modern or fifteenth century workmanship.

A Bessborough gem. Natter (Cat. No. 38) suggests that the eyes were once represented in metal; or, more probably, they contained precious stones that have been removed.

674.—Cameo on yellow sard. A comic mask of second century workmanship.

A Bessborough gem (Cat. No. 40).

675.—Cameo on a white onyx. A small comic mask, probably of Roman workmanship.

GRYLLI, CAPRICES, ETC.

676.—A minute cameo on onyx ; representing a spirited little mask rendered in a red stratum ; the beard being done in a white layer on a dark ground.

One of the Medina gems (Cat. No. 24 M).

677.—Cameo on sardonyx. A mask, cut on a red stratum, the beard being rendered in a white layer on a dark ground, into which the eyes and mouth are cut down. A clever Roman work.

A Medina gem (Cat. No. 26 M).

678.—Cameo on an onyx. A Bacchic mask in which the crown of the head is fractured. An antique work in a white layer, on a yellowish base.

679.—Cameo on a chert-like jasper, 1 inch by ⅞ths ; a stone that occasionally occurs with fine antique work. A front-faced Bacchic mask, in rather low relief. It is a spirited and undoubtedly antique work.

680.—Cameo on an onyx. A mask as of a youthful Bacchus ; over each brow a little spot of red cornelian represents the corymbi. It is a Roman work, cut in a white layer on a red cornelian base.

681.—Cameo on an onyx. Silenus mask, in front-face : a head bound with a fillet with two corymbi. It is an excellent Roman work in flat relief, cut in a white layer on a dark gray base.

682.—Cameo on an onyx. A quite modern mask in very high relief.

683.—Cameo ; a front-face mask. Modern work.

2.—GRYLLI, CAPRICES, &c.

684.—Intaglio on a nicolo. A gryllus, representing a bald Silenus head united at the back with a goat's head. A good Roman work.

One of the Bessborough gems (Cat. No. 67).

685.—Intaglio on jasper, beautifully set. A caprice, in which a Cupid rides a horse, of which only the head and neck are equine, the body being formed of a ram's head eating an ear of corn; the chest is formed by a mask with a projection from the chin, which supports a goat that is disputing with the horse for a wisp of hay; below it is a serpent. The lower part of the design is formed of an eagle tearing a hare, as on the coins of Agrigentum. The work is late and extremely rude.

> This elaborate caprice was one of the Chesterfield gems (Cat. No. 36 c).

686.—Intaglio on a splendid blood sard. A gryllus, in which a peacock and a ram's head are combined with an elephant's head, a serpent, and a Silenus mask. Round it are the letters, ANICE. T. P. S. Fair work of late Roman time.

> One of the Medina gems (Cat. No. 12 M). It was published by Borioni at Rome.

687.—Intaglio on a jasper, carrying a gryllus representing a horse's head and neck, a mask, &c., on cocks' legs. Rude late Roman work.

> An Arundel gem (Cat. Thec. A, No. 34).

688.—Intaglio on a fine nicolo. A gryllus representing an elephant's head ingeniously combined with two masks. A pretty caprice of very nice Roman work.

> An Arundel gem (Cat. Thec. A, No. 66).

689.—Intaglio on a cornelian. A goat, a horse, and a boar united to form a gryllus. A good example of Roman work.

690.—Intaglio on a beryl. A head of Jupiter, perhaps of Jupiter Ammon, united to a ram's head, and with a curved neck over it somewhat like the Egyptian Vulture head-dress; in the beak of the bird's head is a small branch, perhaps of olive. The whole caprice is borne upon a pair of cocks' legs. A work of a good period.

691.—Intaglio on a poor sard. A Siren: a beautifully cut gem of the last century, worthy of Natter.

> One of the Bessborough gems (Cat. No. 108).

3.—ANIMAL FORMS.

692.—Intaglio on a sard. A ram, or Aries as an astronomical symbol, the fleece being burnt white by an artificial process. It is fair Roman work.

693.—Intaglio on an onyx, cut *en cabochon*. A goat browsing on a large ear of corn is engraved in the top layer, of a coral-red colour. The work is of the ordinary Roman type.

694.—Cameo on a very small onyx of two goats, cut in an upper white layer.

    One of the Bessborough gems (Cat. No. 49).

695.—Intaglio on a yellowish sard. A sow: very good work by Marchant.

696.—Intaglio on a banded sard. A bull; a crescent in the field. A nicely executed Roman gem, set in a most handsome ring of the last century, ornamented with twisted vines. It has been wofully re-polished.

    An Arundel gem (Cat. Thec. A, No. 84).

697.—Intaglio on a good sard. A bull, represented, by a Roman artist, in the position of the bull on the coins of Thurium.

698.—Intaglio on a fine golden sard. Four cows; three are standing and one lying down. The surface of the stone has been re-polished, and the gem has the appearance of a work by a good Roman artist.

    An Arundel gem (Cat. Thec. A, No. 70).

699.—Intaglio on a transparent chalcedony. A cow, in very rude and late Roman work.

    Perhaps the Arundel gem (Cat. Thec. A, 69).

114   ANIMAL FORMS.

700.—Intaglio on a poor sard. A cow and calf, of good antique workmanship.

701.—Intaglio on a cornelian. A horse or ass; extremely late and rude Roman work.

Possibly the Arundel gem (Cat. Thec. A, No. 98).

702.—Cameo on an onyx, slightly convex. Two horses; one drinks and the other stands by him. The forms are drawn in beautiful proportion, and it is a work probably by a Greek hand and of high merit.

One of the Arundel gems (Cat. Thec. A, No. 135).

703.—A glass paste copy of the above.

704.—Cameo in an onyx. A chestnut horse, represented in his natural colour in an upper layer of the stone, on a dark base layer. The horse is biting at a fetter. A work, from the treatment of its anatomical detail, attributable to the second century.

705.—Cameo on an onyx. An elephant trampling on a long and large fish which he is goring with his tusks. It is a work remarkable for its spirited character and correct design. Mr. King has ingeniously suggested that it alludes to the fabled combats between elephants and monstrous eels in Indian rivers, recorded by Ctesias. It seems certainly an ancient work.

706.—Cameo on sardonyx. An animal, perhaps a lynx. Cut in a white layer on a brownish red base. Very nice early antique work.

Arundel gem (Ar. Cat. Thec. A, 143).

707.—Cameo, of a poodle or lap-dog. Perhaps Roman.

708.—A cameo, apparently representing two dogs wearing comic masks, and probably a Roman work.

ANIMAL FORMS. 115

709.—Intaglio on a nicolo, representing a fox, in rude Roman work.

  An Arundel gem (Cat. Thee. A, No. 68).

710.—Cameo on a paste in imitation of an onyx. A dog, or perhaps a wolf, lying down, seen from above. Cut in a white layer, by perhaps a Roman hand.

711.—Cameo on an onyx. An animal like a panther; cut in a tawny upper layer, with a mottled black jasper base; the animal is also mottled with spots. The antiquity of the work is extremely doubtful.

  An Arundel gem (Cat. Thee. C, No. 22), formerly united to the gem No. 718.

712.—Cameo on mottled jasper. A panther couchant, seen from above; cut in a brown upper layer mottled with spots, the base being a jasper, reddish and gray. It is a modern work, and is set in a ring with brilliants.

  Purchased for twenty guineas by the third Duke.

713.—Intaglio on a fine almandine garnet. A lion seen in front-face and somewhat foreshortened; his paw on the head of a stag. A dog behind the lion is skulking off, baying. The work is remarkably bold.

  This garnet, No. 57 in Natter's Catalogue, was one of the Bessborough gems. In his Traité, Natter describes and figures (No. xvii.) a similar but less complex gem—a fragment on amethyst—in Lord Carlisle's Collection. Considering the complexity of the subject of this gem, it seems eminently probable that Natter's master hand engraved it as a reproduction, with improvements, of the Carlisle amethyst. The treatment of the head is much like that on the far-famed star-dog Sirius, No. 270 in this Collection, with the *technique* of which Natter says he had acquired familiarity.

714.—Intaglio on a fine plasma. A lion passant, with his foot on a bull's head. A late and rather poor Roman work, symbolical probably of the sun.

715.—Intaglio on a nicolo. A sleeping lion; a well-modelled Roman work.

ANIMAL FORMS.

716.—Cameo on a sardonyx. A very fine cameo of a lion preying on a bull. The lion is in a rich brown upper layer in rather high relief. The bull is rendered in a flat manner in order to take advantage of a thin white layer; the base is dark. The stone has been pierced lengthways by a hole, and another goes through the face of the gem, where a third has also been begun. The work has all the character of genuine antiquity.

Purchased for 50*l*. by the third Duke. See Introduction, p. xvii.

717.—A cameo in bold relief, in cat's eye, representing a lion's head; the chatoyance of the material giving a remarkable life to a work which is otherwise tame. It is by a cinque-cento hand, and is set in a pretty frame formed of golden loops.

See Introduction, p. xvii.

718.—Cameo on sardonyx. A lion passant, his tail curled under the hind leg. This spirited work is cut in a rich brown sard upper layer, with an under layer of white. It is set in a heavy gold mounting, carefully chiselled on the back in the seventeenth century, and similar to that of No. 711. The work is undercut, and like the panther, No. 711, formerly attached to it, it is probably of sixteenth century workmanship.

It was in the Arundel Collection (Cat. Thec. C, No. 22).

719.—Cameo on a jasper-onyx. A lion passant, cut in a tawny brown upper layer supported by a black base. A delicately finished work of the last century.

720.—Intaglio on a sard. Three eagles standing upon three altars: in the very rudest work of the late Roman time.

An Arundel gem (Cat. Thec. A, No. 97).

721.—Intaglio on an onyx. An eagle standing on an altar. Rude work of the second century: cut in a white layer with a black base, and set as a seal with enamelled flowers.

An Arundel gem (Cat. Thec. A, No. 71).

722.—Cameo on an onyx. An eagle and a serpent, on the reverse of No. 586, with the motto "Nihil est quod non tolleret qui perfecte diligit." Beautiful cinque-cento work.

(Bessb. Cat. No. 12).

723.—Intaglio on a chalcedony. A peacock standing on a basket, a raven standing on a cornucopiæ, and a cock between them. A late and rude Roman work.

An Arundel gem (Cat. Thec. A, No. 94).

724.—Intaglio on a nicolo. Representation in late Roman work of a peacock and a cornucopiæ.

An Arundel gem (Cat. Thec. A, No. 96).

725.—Intaglio on a nicolo. A cock with a wreath in his bill. Very rude work, with the word VIGIL written forwards in the exergue.

An Arundel gem (Cat. Thec. A, No. 93).

726.—Intaglio on a sard. An owl standing on a branch. A fine modern work.

A Bessborough gem (Cat. No. 93).

727.—Cameo on an onyx. A quail, as if fighting, in a red layer on a white ground.

A Bessborough gem (Cat. No. 83).

728.—Intaglio on a Siriam garnet. A frog. Fine Roman work.

A Bessborough gem (Cat. No. 87).

729.—Intaglio on a sard. A cicada perched on a caduceus. A delicately worked Roman gem.

730.—Intaglio on a green jasper, with red bands. A scorpion.

An Arundel gem (Cat. Thec. A, 67).

731.—Intaglio on a fine almandine garnet, cut *en cabochon*. A very fine Roman gem, representing a spider in its web.

One of the Medina gems (Cat. No. 48 M).

ANIMAL FORMS.

732.—Cameo on sardonyx. The Œstrus, or horse-fly, most perfectly represented, of the natural size and colour, in a translucent brown layer, supported by a reddish under layer. It is magnificent work of the finest Roman period. One of the wings is slightly broken.

A Medina gem (Cat. No. 27 M).

733.—Cameo on an onyx. A four-winged scarab of Romano-Egyptian work. Cut in a pale brownish layer on a white base.

734.—Intaglio on a fine blue convex aquamarine. A Hippocampus. Beautiful antique work, possibly cut by a Greek hand.

735.—Cameo on an onyx. A Hippocampus cut in a whitish layer with a black base, rather stiffly drawn; in its original gold setting. The work is certainly antique.

A Bessborough gem (Cat. No. 30).

736.—Cameo on an onyx. A Gryphon in a white layer with a brownish base. It is rather nice Roman work.

A Bessborough gem (Cat. No. 82).

737.—Cameo on an onyx. A nondescript animal, the face and different parts being rendered in differently coloured layers of the stone. It is a conceit of the early renaissance period.

738.—Intaglio on an onyx. Capricorn and rudder (?) A very rude Roman work; the signet probably of a sailor.

An Arundel gem (Cat. Thec. A, No. 100).

739.—Intaglio on a banded agate. A dolphin and rudder, of very rude workmanship.

An Arundel gem (Cat. Thec. A, No. 101).

www.ingramcontent.com/pod-product-compliance
Lightning Source LLC
Chambersburg PA
CBHW020853160426
43192CB00007B/902